Mondays in the Middle East

The Lighter Side of Arabian Nights

by

David A. Cross, Jr.

xulon PRESS

To Cheryl
You are my good gift, my Eudora.

Acknowledgements

I want to specially thank Rebecca Blomker and my beloved wife Cheryl for their tireless efforts in editing. You've certainly left your mark in making this work much more than it would have been without you. I'm amazed that a person could make as many mistakes as I did. Any that remain are my own.

A special thanks to Fatima Bin-Thabet as well for her critical reading of the text. Your comments sharpened my sensitivity in editing. Thank you.

Thanks to Russ Lunak whose example of encouragement is a model for me. I appreciate your faithful interest in all that I'm doing and your wise words through the years.

Thanks to Tim, Mike, and Drew for sharing your stories! They're some of the best ones in here.

Most of all, thanks to my Savior who made me all I am today. Eternity is too short when it's spent with you.

To Mom, Penny, Shirley, and all of you who encouraged me to publish these simple stories, thank you. You've challenged me to better things.

εἰς την δοξαν του Θεου
David A. Cross

Foreword

Any group of people with international experience can have an evening filled with laughter by sharing stories of cultural situations, faux pas, differences, language errors, etc. I remember such an evening on the topic of "Toilets we've used." Certainly <u>Mondays in the Middle East</u> provides such fun.

However, that might be the sugar that helps the medicine go down. I'd like to focus attention on the serious contribution David Cross makes in his collection of Monday musings.

Sooner or later in any extended cross-cultural living situation, culture shock becomes an issue. The euphoria of entry-level excitement is soon lost to potentially destructive feelings arising from the differences, the unfamiliar, the misunderstood, and the occasional conflicts. It is not only the bug bites that get under our skin. If ignored, negative reaction to cultural situations can nullify abilities, abort accomplishment, and defeat effectiveness. The very purpose for being in the second culture will not be fulfilled. So how does one deal with culture shock?

Any good international organization will offer training in cross-cultural living as pre-departure preparation. In my first year of international work in Asia I learned quickly that the comfort of the seminar room didn't prepare me adequately for the frequently uncomfortable realities of life in the second culture. I had to cope. I learned coping through 25 years of crossing cultural boundaries in Asia. I incorporated Coping 101 into the unwritten curriculum in the Cultural Anthropology classes I taught for 10 years. Mondays in the Middle East would have been very useful, both personally and as assigned reading for students. By illustration from his experiences, Cross offers the reader effective coping mechanisms using laughter more readily than lecture.

As an undergraduate David Cross enrolled in the Introduction to Cultural Anthropology class I taught. From day one his goal was obvious: cross cultural, international employment. He impressed me with his ability to observe, analyze, and synthesize, to produce meaning and increase understanding. Those abilities are the background to his writing here. And therein lies much of the value of the book. It is an example: deal with culture shock as he does. Observe. Analyze. Synthesize. The result? Cultural incidents lose their threat, ambiguities become less upsetting, and a measure of understanding develops, going beyond mere tolerance of differences to a degree of comfort with them. Process it, don't react to it. Thus, living internationally becomes manageable, productive, and even enjoyable.

Particularly Mondays in the Middle East caught my attention in its use of three coping strategies: humor, comparison, and connection—always without defensiveness. Cross not only finds humor in many situations but, more importantly, he often laughs at himself, not overly serious about ego protection. Further, he copes by comparing the new with the old, finding the comparative elements. Sort of, "Oh. I see, they accomplish 'xyz' this way, we did 'xyz' that way." Cross does that while skillfully avoiding the "we-they" adversarial mentality. Finally, he makes connections between the unfamiliar (the new culture) and the familiar (the home culture), which defuses the cultural incident. He finds common denominators rather than abrasive discontinuities.

I wish that 30 years ago I had used those mechanisms more effectively. But I did not employ the most important lesson in <u>Mondays in the Middle East</u>: Do your own "Monday musings." Create your time for cultural reflection to tune harmoniously into your new world. Following Cross's example will be useful in the process of becoming comfortable and effective in the new cultural setting. Enjoy the reading but take seriously his coping mechanisms.

Russell Lunak
Professor Emeritus
International Business
Northwestern College
St. Paul, Minnesota

Arabian Nights 101

It was a perfect night for a walk after the blistering sun finally made its transit to the other side of the Atlantic. I stepped out of my home in the village of Buraimi, Oman, onto a dirt and gravel road beneath my feet. The crunching sound of the gravel on such a serene night added to the picturesque atmosphere. I said to myself, "Ahh, now this is Arabia."

Whether I need the exercise or not, evening walks give my cell phone a chance to catch up on the day's SMS messages. Sometimes I question whether a cell phone defeats the purpose when weak signals in my desert village prevent me from using the thing in my own home. Even these tiny text messages can't get through, but at least they will wait until I step outside and get a signal. Pity those poor unfortunate souls trying to call me through the day. Memorizing the Arabic and English answering message would be a snap: "We're sorry. The number you have called is either switched off or moved out of the coverage area." Well, at least they can resort to writing SMS text messages to say, "Why don't you ever have a cell phone signal?"

Nonetheless, this is all a good excuse for a relaxing walk. Our village is located right on the Tropic of Cancer, so by around 5 p.m. the land goes dark and the stars come out in force. Being that close to the equator lends to an earlier sunset in summer. Surprisingly, our latitude even changes the shape of the moon. Instead of the crescent moon looking like a strong, proud capital 'C,' its new horseshoe 'U' look makes it seem like the poor thing just had a fender bender with an asteroid and it's barely hanging on for dear life.

This particular night was no exception to the heavenly anomalies, and the lack of street lights throughout my neighborhood intensified the crisp contrast of the stars against a pitch black sky. As I walked along, however, I noticed a strange blue light off in the distance. As I walked closer I could see this azure-blue orb swinging back and forth, back and forth, almost as though it were on some sort of pendulum about seven feet off the ground. What was even more odd about this is that the alien light was swinging in the middle of the roadway which made my curiosity all the more intense. Moving closer and closer, I began to make out the shape of a man standing beneath this oscillating luminosity, seemingly entranced by its radiance just as I was. What was this mysterious light floating above the earth, disrupting the tranquility of the night? None other than a pitiful cell phone user like myself standing in the deserts of Arabia waving his phone high above his head vainly seeking even one bar on his LCD panel indicating some sort of phone signal.

Welcome to Arabia where East meets West and old meets new. It's a land of clashing cultures and changing times where families of camel herders fifty years ago are mastering fiber-optic infrastructure and lucrative petrochemical engineering. Even in the midst of all of this change, the traditional Arab way of life somehow lives on. You might not recognize them at first glance, but the mystery and nostalgia of Arabia are still there beneath the precarious balance of tradition and progress.

If anything, Mondays in the Middle East is an invitation to explore this mystery and nostalgia. I began writing these explorations into culture in 1999 while living in the small island nation of Bahrain in the Arabian (Persian) Gulf. Some of those early stories are included here as "Flashbacks," either in the related time of year, or the related subject. Otherwise, you'll find a chronological ordering of weekly entries from 2004-2006. I sent those updates to friends each week by email, and I found that the writing turned out to be quite a bit of fun.

From the beginning, these simple stories had two aims: educate and entertain. I set out to give people a perspective on the Middle East that they don't get in the mainstream media. It seems that many Westerners think every Arab carries an AK-47 and a hand grenade, but I want to present some of the real-life situations I've come across that present a different view and I want to do it with a bit of humor for all.

"Toto, I don't think we're in Kansas anymore." You can say that again. We're not even in the Midwest; but we're about to arrive in the Middle East, so sit back and enjoy the ride! And if you see anything strange in the Arabian night air, just take a moment to step back and ponder. You might have a good laugh, but you'll certainly come away with something to remember. After all, it's not every night that you see an alien blue light hovering over the ground in the still, desert air. Here, that's just another Monday in the Middle East.

D.A.C.
August 2006

December 13, 2004 –
The Second Left Past the Camel Market

Driving directions are always tricky in different parts of the U.S. Some people are so prepared that they email maps in advance. Some people give street names with left-right directions and some give landmark directions. Some even give landmark directions with a helpful "you can't miss it" disclaimer.

Here in the Middle East, people generally fall into the *landmark/"you can't miss it"* variety, except an Arabic phrase makes them the *landmark/"In Sha Allah"* variety. *"In Sha Allah"* technically means "if God wills it" but often it's just used as "hopefully." After I received some directions today, my friend finished with the confidence-inspiring phrase, *"In Sha Allah*, you'll find your way back to my house." Hmmm, now was that "if God wills it" or was it "hopefully"? Will I see my family again or will I wander aimlessly through the Arabian Peninsula until my beard is as long as this story?

Maybe the landmark directions will be clear enough. After all, I was even given a map, and maps are pretty clear, right? On the other hand, the map's landmarks were things like "big house" and "coffee pot" and "sports club." With very few road signs here, I can understand that there really is no choice but to give landmark directions, but how descript is "big house"? Is that before or after "big mosque"? Should I stop at the stop sign that slid down the pole to the ground? Maybe I should just follow the car in front of me and drive across the field before I reach the intersection.

As it turned out, landmark directions were just fine and I felt like I was back in rural Wisconsin: "Oh, just go up past the big red barn about a mile or so, take a left after the fresh cut corn field, then a right after the old plow out in the alfalfa field. You'll find it." *In Sha Allah.*

Life is different here, and that's just another Monday in the Middle East.

December 20, 2004 – Strapped In

I had to laugh at myself today because I went out and bought a new pair of sandals. It wasn't that I lacked sandals. No, I actually bought some sandals about a year and a half ago to prepare to come here and I really like those sandals. Then I got here and found they really aren't as convenient as one would think because of the strap around the heel. So I bought some with no strap around the heel.

Why would I need those? To enter people's homes, of course! It's customary to remove your shoes as you enter a home, even if you only enter for a minute or two, but it can be clumsy. For example, I walked over to a friend's shop/home, took my shoes off for a two minute visit, put my shoes back on to walk across the street, took them off again for another three or four minute stop, put them back on again to return to the shop, took them off again . . . . You get the idea. Sandals with straps to unbuckle were simply too awkward which is something I should have known.

At least they're cheap, though. A while back my uncle jested to me, "I bet you paid full price for those half-shoes, didn't ya? They really saw you coming!" In this case, I paid about half price for the "half-shoes." Not bad. Not bad for another Monday in the Middle East.

December 27, 2004 –
Possession is Nine-tenths of the law.

Ownership is an interesting concept here in the Gulf. We've just recently bought a car from someone who didn't own it. By the way, we don't own it either. Peculiar, wouldn't you say?

As it happens, only residents can own vehicles, but I'm not a resident. I'm just a visitor. So was the gentleman who sold the car to me. In fact, the owner bought the car but never used it. He just sold it to the man who didn't own it.

When I think about it, I guess I could say that it's the most expensive car I've never owned . . . I think. Then again, I've never owned a Corvette, but I've never bought a Corvette I didn't own, either. Is your mind reeling yet? I'm not sure if I'll ever figure this one out which makes this one more reason life is different here, and that's just another Monday in the Middle East.

January 3, 2005 – Getting Powered Up

A friend told me the other day, "You are almost certainly the only person in the country with a snowman in your living room." I suppose in a land where a winter cold spell means highs in the 60's, he's probably right. The funny part is how the snowman got there.

Before we left for the Middle East I got an inflatable snowman as a gift and I brought it along thinking, "This will be great! I'll blow it up for the Christmas party in the desert we'll be going to!" I didn't even bother to open it or look at it; otherwise I might have decided to leave it home.

It turns out, it isn't "inflatable" in the mouth-to-nozzle variety, but it runs an electric fan to inflate it, and it must remain plugged in to remain inflated. So much for the Christmas party in the desert. Not only that, it is a good old 110-volt two-prong American-style electrical plug. Neither the 110-volt nor the American two-prong works well with the huge three-prong British sockets for 220-volt electricity here.

Never fear! I located a two-prong European-style voltage converter. Now I can plug my two-prong American-style 110-volt snowman into the 220-volt two-prong European-style converter which is plugged into the three-prong British adapter here. All of that to run a very foreign inflatable snowman right here in my living room in the Middle East! Ahh, the wonders of technology and the wonders of another Monday in the Middle East.

January 10, 2005 – Arab Hospitality

I'm not sure if it is because of the heat in the region or just general Arab hospitality, but you are always to offer guests some sort of drink at your home. This hospitality isn't just for invited guests, but it's even for plumbers, electricians, and any workmen in your home. Everyone should be offered a Pepsi, a Dew, or whatever.

Recently, a friend and I hired some men for an hour and a half to move a washer and some bookshelves that we'd purchased. They drove their truck with us, loaded the furniture, drove to our home, unloaded the furniture and put it in place. However, the washer was too big to fit through the bathroom door, but it fit into another bathroom with a 1/4 inch wider door. Even this was with some labor, though, as the workers were forced to unscrew the door from its hinges, put the washer in the bathroom, and reattach the door.

All the while that they were doing all of this, I searched our house, but found none of the expected drinks of Pepsi, Coke, or any other canned beverage. At the end of an hour and 20 minutes or so my friend offered them the agreed payment, but they refused! "We need more for the extra work," they complained.

My friend asserted, "You agreed on this price for an hour-and-a-half's work!"

"No, no," they objected. "We moved everything and we took off the door and put it back on. We did all this extra work and with no Pepsi!"

I'm more prepared now; I bought a case of Pepsi to keep on hand. I guess that's cheaper than paying for more than a case of it when the workers complain of "no Pepsi!" Thirst is universal, but life is different here, and that's just another Monday in the Middle East.

January 17, 2005 – Black and White at the Zoo

I have to confess the theft of the following phrase from a good friend: "In this country, men and women are as different as black and white!"

This is said tongue-in-cheek, referring to the typical Arab style of dress. Traditional women wear black *abayyas* that completely cover their bodies from head to toe, and the men wear white *kandura*s from the neck down and usually a red and white checkered head covering. Of course, there's special dispensation for the occasional modern youth gussied up with a Chicago Cubs baseball hat. It's an odd sort of anachronism to see someone in a traditional white *kandura* wearing a Cubs baseball cap with a cell phone stuck to his ear!

Kanduras can be dangerous, though. While at the zoo recently we watched a couple of hippos happily chomp away on a lunch of cucumbers, carrots, and heads of lettuce. Meanwhile, a man wearing a white *kandura* stepped right up to the fence with his family to get a closer view of the hippos.

Without breaking the rhythmic chomping of its jowls, one of the hippos began to rid itself of "excess" from the other end, first in liquid form, then the whole package. In very efficient fashion, the hippo slapped its short, stubby tail back and forth during the process to clear the "excess" from its rear, much to the chagrin of the man in the all-white *kandura* standing only a few feet away! Who needs a manure spreader when you've got a power tail like that! It was an interesting Arabic lesson about what is said and done in not-so-pleasant circumstances. Actually, this gentleman handled it quite well with a grain of humor in the presence of his children and a sympathetic audience of an American family. At least a cow raises its tail in warning, but not so with the hippo!

Just to be on the safe side, I think I'll wear camouflage to the zoo next time. It's a different life – full of surprises, but it's still just another Monday in the Middle East.

January 24, 2005 –
One Man's Junk is Another Man's Treasure
In junior high school I found myself getting into quite a bit of mischief, and one of those mischievous activities was "Dumpster Diving." I understand now that this sort of practice is against the law, but back then we were simply amazed

at all the good junk we could find in dumpsters, especially at businesses. To them, it was junk, but to us, we had visions of building ultra secret spy gadgets and all sorts of techno-wizardry. Imagine what we could contrive with an assortment of floppy drives, ribbon cables and shelving units. We were on our way to the moon!

This week, however, was not the week for dumpster diving in the Middle East. This week, Muslims celebrated *Eid Al Adha* which is the holiday to remember Abraham's willingness to sacrifice his son. To commemorate this, families that can afford it slaughter a sheep or a goat. It's important to clarify that they don't take it to a butcher, but they slaughter it themselves. So, in cities like Dubai, police gave out citations for the mess that the slaughtering made. Don't worry, though, the police gave clemency with all those citations; all fines were forgiven as a gesture to celebrate the *Eid* holiday.

In small villages like mine, an overpowering stench settled over the neighborhood from all the animal remains in the dumpsters, or out of the dumpsters, as the case may be. My macabre discovery this week was an animal leg lying outside the fly-infested dumpster. For most people, that's not the sort of thing to write home about, but for me it's just another Monday in the Middle East.

Flashback!
July 12, 1999 – Smuggling Coke

Ah, yes, this time of year is a good time to tip back a nice cola with a victorious sneer at the hot sun. Many people say that ANY time of year is a good time to tip back a nice cola. In Muslim countries, though, that is not the thing to do during the fasting hours of the month of Ramadan. If you are unfamiliar with Ramadan, it is the month that Muslims refrain from eating, drinking, and smoking during daylight hours. Some religious leaders even teach that swallowing is forbidden which gives rise to spitting indoors and outdoors by men and women. Interesting. All things considered, even foreigners or non-Muslims can't eat or drink in public during the hours of fasting.

When Ramadan came around this past year we experienced its challenges first hand. For my wife, Ramadan was especially difficult because she teaches at an Arab school. Basically, she was forced to fast even though she's not a Muslim. Oh, there did come those days, though, when she desperately wanted even water to drink, but wow, how exhilarating a Coca-Cola would be! On those days she snuck across the street to buy a nice cola and hid it until she could get someplace private like a bathroom stall. Taking care to muffle the "Psst" as she opened it, she furtively tipped it back and found it . . . ahhh, delicious and refreshing! Perhaps now she should write a book entitled "Ramadan Smuggler." Life is different here, and that's just another Monday in the Middle East.

January 31, 2005 – Stuffed Crust Pizza

For as much as they hate pork in this part of the world, they sure love other sausages. Every grocery store seems to have a wide selection of chicken hot dogs, turkey hot dogs, and beef hot dogs, and I found out tonight that even pizza joints have hot dogs.

Tonight we went out to eat at one of the three Pizza Huts in town, and my wife ordered a sausage and pepperoni pizza with stuffed crust. Being a Wisconsin boy, I consider the invention of a cheese-filled crust to be one of the greatest concoctions in pizza. Who can resist biting into a soft tunnel of bread filled with stringy mozzarella cheese?

This stuffed crust pizza, however, gave new meaning to "stuffed crust." I ate down to the crust of my first piece of pizza and chomped in expecting a stretchy piece of cheese to delight my tastes. Instead, I said to my wife, "This tastes like hot dog!" After a few more bites, I became absolutely convinced and I tore open the remaining crust for further investigation. She was certainly humored when I pulled out a full hot dog from the crust of my pizza (minus three bites)!

I think next time I order a sausage and pepperoni pizza with stuffed crust, I'll have to clarify that the sausage is to be on the pizza and the crust is to be stuffed with CHEESE. Come to think of it, skip the hot dog. I'll just have pepperoni. Ahh yes, life is different here, and that's just another Monday in the Middle East.

February 7, 2005 – The Story of the Starving Ecologist

It's another Monday in the Middle East where I am enjoying a sunny day of 84 degrees this February 7. The weather is pretty consistent for about three months of the year, then totally predictable for the other nine. From December through February, the weather will be sunny with highs in the mid-70's to mid-80's followed by nine months of sunny skies with temperatures between 90 and 120. Hey, I could be a weather forecaster.

However, I was struck by a thought recently: If this country can employ a meteorologist for a forecast this simple, it should be able to employ the poor starving ecologists. OK, OK, it's only an assumption, but I am assuming that the ecologists and environmentalists in this country are starving because they sure aren't working!

Here's a story of one starving ecologist. As I was driving along the highway, I observed something I have only seen here in the Middle East. A man had pulled over his car to the side of the road and he was literally bailing out the trash onto the roadside! With three kids I know that our car gets pretty messy, but judging by the bucket loads of trash he was emptying onto the gravel, I'm guessing he had at least eight or ten kids under the age of four.

Here's another story of an ecologist on the slopes to poverty. There is this mindset here that absolutely everything needs a plastic bag. "Oh, is that a stick of gum you bought? Let me get a one-gallon plastic bag for you." I went to the store the other day for groceries and I got 21 plastic bags with my $100 of groceries! They even bagged the wooden crate of oranges I bought. "Are you buying a bag of diapers that already has a carrying handle on it? Let's bag that thing all by itself."

Another time I bought a new mop, and they put a plastic bag around the mop head so that I could leave the store in style like a truly proud owner of a new mop. I felt like a fisherman with a trophy walleye hanging from my rod.

I bought some large sheets of drafting paper the other day and I didn't need anyone to translate the look on the clerk's face which said, "Do you want me to go to the back room and get a plastic bag for these two-foot by three-foot sheets of paper?" No thanks, I'll just carry them with my own two hands. Oh, the novelty of life, where that's just another Monday in the Middle East.

February 14, 2005 – Donut Profiling

Where we lived in the States, my skin color is in the majority, but in the Middle East I can be spotted in a crowd from a mile away. This comes with its advantages and disadvantages. As for an advantage, I can walk into any Western hotel, sit down in the lobby, and enjoy some nice reading time without being asked why I'm there. As for a disadvantage, I pay a higher price for everything where bartering might be involved. Discrimination is no secret here. There's even an accepted pay scale that is published in business magazines which lays out the expected salary rates for different nationalities for the same job. Arab nationals get the highest salary, then Westerners, then Asians, then Indians. It's open discrimination, but it's openly accepted by everyone.

Of all the places to find racial profiling, though, I didn't expect it at Dunkin' Donuts. A few weeks ago I bought some donuts and while I was waiting for them to be bagged up, I looked over my receipt. Interestingly, I noticed a line, "1 U.S./U.K." I asked the gentleman what this meant and he replied, "You are from the U.S. or U.K., right?"

"Yes," I answered, "but why is it on my receipt? Do you keep track of nationalities of customers?" He answered, yes, as though there was nothing strange about that.

I could tell my question was strange to him, though, because the next time I went into the shop, he remembered me. That's right, I'm the white guy who's in on the Dunkin' Donut secret: racial profiling over donuts! What can I say? Life is different here, and that's just another Monday in the Middle East.

February 21, 2005 – Many Refrigerators

Weather is a common topic of conversation anywhere. From the frozen tundra of Lambeau Field to the frozen air conditioners of the Middle East, you can always resort to weather when you run out of things to say.

In arid climates like the Middle East, engineers have to manufacture different climates in order to enjoy the activities of the rest of the world. For instance, our nearby mall is the most extravagant mall I've ever seen, complete with a year-round indoor ice rink. Not only that, but Arabs don't want to be excluded from the joys of downhill skiing, so a building in Dubai now hosts a man-made mountain. That's right, there's a 1,000 foot *indoor* ski slope.

Leave it to me, though, to manufacture not only weather, but strange conversation about weather. Shortly after we arrived in this country, I was talking in Arabic with one of my neighbors about the weather here compared to the weather in the United States. I was trying to make a good impression since I'd only met the man once previously and I generally feel that great emotion in speaking helps to communicate the point. This conversation was no exception. With great enthusiasm and hand gestures I explained, "There is a LOT of snow in America this time of year! There is three feet of snow on the ground!" With much grace and a little laughter, my Arab neighbor kindly corrected my Arabic because what I actually said was, "There are many REFRIGERATORS in America this time of year! There is even a three foot refrigerator on the ground!" Remember, life is different here, and that's just another Monday in the Middle East.

Flashback!
February 22, 1999 – Gird Your Loins

There's a lesson about ice cream that every child learns very quickly. This desert land teaches this lesson especially well with summer temperatures around 110-120 degrees daily. All brands of ice cream make a speedy transition to "soft serve," and the white, sugary soup draining down my arm proves it. How can I fight that sort of fiery heat? How can I get my box of Bresler's home before the Neapolitan becomes brown slush? Fight fire with ice and pack your own cooler of Antarctica to the grocery store. That's how!

Needless to say, with that kind of heat I didn't expect to find an ice rink in Bahrain. Nonetheless, there is a well used indoor rink, and I've done more skating here in six months than in the last two years back in Minnesota. Westerners aren't the only ones giving ice skating a try, but the local skaters have an interesting modesty dilemma to overcome in order to enjoy the cooler world of recreation. As you may know, traditional clothing for men is a one-piece robe from shoulders to floor that might normally hinder ice skating, but not in Bahrain! Here the men just grab the bottom of the robe, pull it up between their legs, tie it in a knot at the waist, and carry on skating without even stumbling around the rink! Well, at least they don't stumble because of the robe. Life is different here, and that's just another Monday in the Middle East.

February 28, 2005 – No Place Like Home

Normally in the Middle East I take my car to an authorized dealer repair shop, but a few weeks ago I needed repair on a holiday and I couldn't wait until the shop opened the next day. Fortunately for me, I live on a border, so I asked a friend if he would be willing to take me to the repair shop he frequents in the neighboring country since it wasn't a holiday there.

As we were driving to the garage, my friend issued a disclaimer saying, "I have to warn you about this shop that, although they do great work and it is very cheap, it doesn't exactly meet US or UK safety codes. We're talking dirt floors with cars and parts of cars scattered all over the place!" Little did he realize how much this shop would remind me of my grandpa's farm back in Wisconsin. Dirt floors were all too familiar. Cars everywhere for spare parts reminded me of my childhood. Even when neighboring shop workers came over to help diagnose the problem, the whole scenario reminded me of my uncles and my great uncles huddled with my grandpa around a jacked up vehicle with the hood open. Honestly, it was a bit refreshing.

Reminiscing like that was even more refreshing after what happened yesterday. I took my limping vehicle to the "authorized" dealer repair shop for a major transmission problem, and the mechanics were quick to conclude that I needed to replace or rebuild the transmission. That wasn't exactly the refreshing part! After I got their analysis, I took the vehicle across the border where they took a more thorough look and said, "Here's a temporary work-around for the transmission, but the big problem is that you're leaking oil badly. We should fix that first." When I looked at the leak, I agreed, so they went to work.

I returned later that evening and my new friend at the shop said, "These pipes for the oil cooler were broken. New replacements would have cost over $200, but I had a neighbor machinist fashion new pipes for you for $30. My labor charge is $25, which brings the total to $55." Fantastic! Again, I could just picture the welding and pipe bending taking place in my grandpa's tool shed. To top it all off, the owner of the shop said, "If you have any more problems with the car, just bring it here. Even if you don't have money to pay, bring it here. You can pay me after 2-3 months if necessary."

Now, where would you hear that in the U.S.? I'll tell you one place—at the end of Banner Road, Mt. Calvary, Wisconsin. Life is different here. Life is the same here. That's just another Monday in the Middle East.

March 7, 2005 – A Spiritually-Minded Country
Any American coming to this part of the world would likely be surprised at how easy it is to get around since English is so readily available. For instance, most of the road signs and even the license plates are in Arabic and English.

Of course, as an American I only see the English most of the time. My eyes simply aren't trained to read the Arabic, so they naturally gravitate to the English. Recently, though, I've been training my eyes to see the Arabic as I try to spell out the words and make sense of them. I can just imagine what I look like sticking my head out the window trying to spell out a car dealer's sign: T—O—Y—O—T—A. Toyota! I feel like a five-year-old learning to read again, and I'm probably driving like one, too!

Recently I was zipping along at 75 mph (yes, that's the speed limit) on a major highway, and I noticed some signs that are *only* in Arabic! "Hmm, very intriguing. What are these secret messages only for Arabic readers? What's the mystery?" Interestingly, the signs are all spiritual messages like "God is great!" or "God is most high!" or "Praise God!" or "Remember God!" I thought to myself, well, that's kind of uplifting! Then again, maybe it's a bit dangerous, at least for me. When some Westerner is painstakingly laboring to read Arabic signs while driving at 75 mph, I imagine the statistical likelihood of an accident rises sharply. That being said, if I'm going to meet my Maker through a car accident, I can't think of any message I'd rather have in my mind than "God is great!" or "Praise God!" or "God is most high!" Maybe that's just the point; if you get in an accident, the department of transportation wants one of these messages to be the last thing that goes through your mind. I don't know if I should be comforted by that or if I should stick to walking.

Either way, I have to smile each time I see another sign. You're familiar with the "NO-U-TURN" symbol? Picture that on a sign with the Arabic words "Praise God!" written above. "Praise God! No U turns!" Life is different here, and that's just another Monday in the Middle East.

Flashback!
March 8, 1999 – What a Waste

Right now in Bahrain we are basking in 80 degree weather. However, not everything this country has to offer is so pleasant. For instance, Bahrain has a high population of stray cats, and these aristo-cats treat the city like their own personal litter box. Unfortunately, I am greeted by the smell of this litter box on the simplest walk outside our house. On account of this, I was really looking forward to our vacation this past month to France just to escape the smell. Imagine it! The fresh air of a clean city with the sound of a spring-water fountain in the background. I couldn't wait.

Much to my chagrin I discovered the habits of the French regarding their pets. They take their dogs with them everywhere they go, whether it be grocery stores or restaurants. Of course, this comes with the side effect of the sight and smell of these "waste products" left behind all over the sidewalks. I've escaped the litter box and jumped into a kennel! Woe is me! How I long for ordinary life in Wisconsin! Then again, I can't say much for the freshly fertilized fields of the Midwest. Life is different here, and that's just another Monday in the Middle East.

March 14, 2005 –
Eagerly Awaiting the Blistering Heat of Summer

The summer heat here is intense. There's no way around it. When my wife and I first arrived in the Arabian Peninsula, we were greeted with a stifling wall of 107 degree heat and 100% humidity. Oh yeah, we landed at 2 a.m.

The crazy thing is, I can't wait for the summer heat! This takes a bit of explanation, though. You see, each bathroom and kitchen has its own 10-15 gallon electric water heater rather than one central water heater for the whole house. This way, the heaters can easily be switched on or off as needed.

The electric water heaters, however, operate much like your common coffee maker; boil the water and let it cool to desired temperature. So we get scalding water every time with the hot faucet, and everyone in our family has suffered painful minor burns. This being said, my curiosity was burning to know just how hot the water actually is since recommended temperature is 120 degrees and third degree burns can occur within two seconds at 150 degrees. I used a simple candy thermometer which revealed an astounding 195 degrees out of the tap! (Yes, boiling is 212!)

I had to laugh, though, when I found out the real temperature of the tap water considering that I just cooked supper. "Heat the frying oil with medium heat to 180 degrees." Next time I'm in a hurry for supper, I think I'll cook my chicken in tap water instead of frying oil.

Water that hot makes me look forward to the summer when we'll shut off the water heaters all together. Who needs them when even the "cold" tap water is 120 degrees? The only problem is that a cold water shower is *never* an option. Oh well! It's better than burns.

Life is just plain different here, and that's another Monday in the Middle East.

Flashback!
March 22, 1999 – Beware the Secret Family Name

The people of the Middle East take tremendous pride in the honor of their family's name. For example, my friend Sameh was very western in his speech and conduct, but when I asked him if he knew his father's father's father, he recited the previous 12 generations off the top of his head!

The Arab naming system itself can be rather confusing for the western mind. Traditionally, the first-born son of every family is named Mohammed, but he is often called by his second name to distinguish him from his six cousins who might also be named Mohammed. Pity the poor school teacher such as my wife, Cheryl, who has 14 Mohammeds in the same classroom!

Teaching in an Arab school has taught her a number of lessons, too. For instance, a different substitute system challenges her teaching and challenges her with names as well. The system works like this: If a teacher is absent, other teachers take turns teaching the vacated classes during their free periods. Who needs a prep period anyway? A few days ago Cheryl was substituting in a certain class when one boy helpfully volunteered the name of another boy, "His name is KHADISH." Now any teacher worth her salt would at least see this as suspect because if she calls that boy by the name Khadish, she has to wonder: is she calling him by the venerated name of his great-grandfather or is she saying, "Donkey, please take out your pencil and paper"? Fortunately, she didn't commit herself to this blunder but skirted around using the name directly. Life is different here, and that's just another Monday in the Middle East.

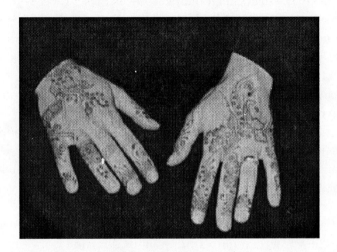

March 21, 2005 – Be Careful What You Read!

I love to write, but I especially love to write letters. There is something special about receiving mail–not just email, but real post. In trying to capture some of the heritage of writing, I even made my own ink this past fall from crushed, boiled walnut shells. My only complaint was that I couldn't really get the ink to be dark enough.

Another natural ink in this part of the world is *henna* and it is used for ornate drawings on women's hands and feet. Such things as nail polish are not religiously permissible because they are not natural, but *henna* trees are natural, so *henna* provides a real social function here. At every special occasion, women get together to adorn their hands with beautiful designs and shapes. The designs typically last a week or two before they fade too much to be seen, but some *henna* seems to be of an extra high quality. This special *henna* goes on much darker and stays on much longer.   M   y wife recently celebrated with a friend who used some of this richer quality *henna* and she happened upon the secret that is behind its composition. Drum roll please. The ancient secret of the beauty of Arab women's hands is diesel fuel! Yep, just mix a bit of diesel fuel with plain old *henna* and you've got the good stuff. I'm not sure how this passes the "natural" test, but it sure works well! Just keep the "NO SMOKING" sign handy for those *henna* parties.

So, if you receive any letters from me with a strange pungent odor, read with caution. I might just be applying Arab wisdom to my homemade ink! Life is different here, and that's just another Monday in the Middle East.

March 28, 2005 –
Honeycombs and Other Breakfast Stories.

Before embarking on this foreign adventure we were warned that we should keep our eyes open for very important signs. For instance, near coastal areas we should know the symptoms for malaria and respond immediately with medical attention. In desert areas, we should be able to recognize the bite of a black widow spider, and so on.

A sign I wasn't expecting to learn is honeycombs. I should explain that these honeycombs aren't exactly your bees-and-honey breakfast cereal, but more of the termite brand breakfast cereal. These little insects will chomp their way in and out of your kitchen table until it resembles Swiss cheese more than fine dining. The previous occupants of our apartment noticed honeycombs gradually growing on a wooden doorframe and they quickly applied the local remedy of diesel fuel. They confided to us that this is not the best aroma to grace a sleeping area, but it was, nonetheless, effective!

Our honeycomb appeared on a brand new piece of furniture. I guess the cherry wood was a tasty appetizer because we would find a fresh pile of, shall we say, termite "waste" beneath the little holes of the honeycomb every few days. A bit of Internet research explained more about these costly pests and their droppings than I ever wanted to know. Lord willing, they were contained to that one piece of furniture which we've replaced. Hey, at least the house isn't a wooden frame! Life is different here, and that's just another Monday in the Middle East.

Flashback!
April 5, 1999 – P-B-and-J

You'd think in coming to an Arab land one of the most difficult adjustments would be the language barrier, and that is true. There are different pronunciations, different emphases on words, and some people just plain jabber a whole lot faster than others. To be sure, we've dealt with the language barrier, and let me tell you, learning British English isn't easy! Oh, the Arabic is all right since I'd expect Arabs not to understand me, but when I talk to my British, Australian, New Zealand, or South African friends I assume we're speaking the same language. "You are speaking English, aren't you? This is your mother tongue, isn't it?" To give you a small example of my travails in speaking English, consider this: If I ask these friends for some jelly they will give me jell-O. If they ask for jam, I would naturally give them jam, not jelly, which is what they asked for. If I ask for preserves, all I get is a bewildered look like I'm asking for caviar on a saltine. Now this is the funny part. Several of our friends heard us Americans rave about peanut butter and jelly sandwiches, so they made themselves sandwiches to give it a try. Naturally, they put some peanut butter on the bread, then they pulled out the jell-O which is what they call "jelly," sloshed it all together in a sandwich and *voila!* They chomped into their first taste of peanut butter and…jell-O!

Ah, yes, life is different here, and that is just another Monday in the Middle East.

April 4, 2005 – *Usmet*

In visiting other cultures, I'm never surprised at the language blunders I see. For instance, in Arabic there is no 'p' sound, so "Pepsi" becomes "*Bibzi.*" Or yesterday, someone at a drive-thru pointed ahead of my car and said, "Bark there." Ruff, Ruff.

Here's another good one. The sign over a shop says, "Oasis for Textiles and Profane." Hmm, profane textiles?

The winner, though, has to be the "Women's Sliming Centre." Come get slimed up for summer! Want to fit into that swimsuit from last year? Nothing that a little "sliming" won't cure. What a difference one 'm' makes in a word, huh?

Reading these bloopers is one thing, but speaking them is quite another endeavor requiring a unique skill that I have in excess. The other day at the corner store I went in to buy milk and a Snickers bar which is pretty routine for me. I was taken aback a bit by extra conversation in Arabic from the Indian shopkeeper. Try as I might, though, I had to explain to him that I just couldn't understand what he was trying to say, but he kept repeating it, "*USmet!* In house! *USmet!*" After about the fifth or sixth attempt, I simply said, "I'm sorry, but I don't understand," and started to walk out of the store. Then he answered as clear as a bell in perfect English, "You don't understand Arabic. You don't understand English. What do you understand??"

Ahh, sweet humility. There's nothing quite like it! His little aside had the particular knack of dashing to pieces any confidence in Arabic I might have had. But why stop there? This had the particular knack of dashing to pieces any confidence in English I might have had!

In the end, I discovered that the kindly shopkeeper was trying to ask if I needed cleaning in my house – House Maid! You can see the connection can't you? Yes, life is different. Life is good, and that's just another Monday in the Middle East.

Flashback!
April 12, 1999 – Let's see those pearly whites!

I visited the Bahrain National Museum some time ago, and I was impressed with more than just the beautiful architecture of the building. I learned how pearl diving has been the greatest source of income for this tiny island nation literally for thousands of years before the discovery of oil sixty-some years ago. The whole community was built around divers taking months-long trips off shore to pop open the oysters with the most primitive equipment.

Even so, I found the display of an archeological site to be most interesting. One certain part of the display showed burial mounds that dated all the way back to the time of Abraham and I'm not talking about Lincoln! Inside the burial mound was a skeleton at least four thousand years old. Still, archeologists were able to estimate that the girl was in her teens. How did they do that, you ask? Tooth decay! Residents of Bahrain in those days ate primarily dates from date palms with a little fish mixed into their diet here and there. That high volume of sugar in the dates provided consumers with some serious tooth decay, minus the brushing, rinsing, and flossing you do each day. Since the archeologists could see that she had adult teeth but little decay, it makes sense that she was quite young when she died. Keep that in mind next time you choose your toothpaste; someone may be looking at your teeth 4,000 years from now! At least they do that here, but life is different here, and that's just another Monday in the Middle East.

April 11, 2005 – All Creatures of the Earth, Part 1

Recently, someone asked me if we had any pets here in the Middle East. Well, not really. "Isn't that a yes/no question?" I suppose it is, but my answer is more "pest" than "pets."

[The Scene]: I had just shut down the computer and gone to bed. No sooner had I pulled over the covers than I remembered something I needed to do on the computer. So I went back into the living room and switched on the light only to find a nasty three-inch cockroach training for the ten-meter dash. I spun around looking for a shoe or some sort of whipping stick to clobber the thing but I lost track of it by the time I grabbed my hiking boot. "Where did it go?? I know it was going toward the computer, but it's gone!"

[Enter Inspector Cross, city police]: Cockroaches like dark places. It must be hiding some place dark.

So I got down on my knees and inspected all around the nest of cables and book bags beside the computer. Nothing.

Stop! Hey, what's that sound? It's that wretched roach inside my subwoofer! How am I going to fit my size 10 into the subwoofer to teach that thing a lesson? Aha! Duct tape! Hey, if I can't get it out, I'll at least keep it in 'til I can come up with a plan!

Again, I whirled around and ran to the kitchen. I returned to duct tape all the holes in the subwoofer and then sat down to think in safety from the attack of the disgusting-creature genus. Now what? Hmmm. I guess I hadn't planned this far. Hmmm. There it is, scratching away. Hmmm. There it is pushing against the duct tape. OK, now pity is starting to weigh on me for a dirty cockroach!

In the end, I came up with the plan the next day to buy some roach spray and finish it off a bit more humanely than starvation. Thank you, Raid. Now just remember, a roach is more than just a roach; add a little duct tape and you've got a great story for another Monday in the Middle East!

April 18, 2005 – All Creatures of the Earth, Part 2

I found a spider behind the fridge the other day. Not to worry, though, it was a dead one. On the other hand, my mind is a bit edgy nowadays. Was that really a poisonous brown recluse spider with a violin shape on its back? Ahh, it's too shriveled up to tell. I guess it's not much of a threat to me now.

Speaking of spiders and poisons, though, reminds me of a chat I had with a friend. I mentioned that I'd learned scorpions were something to beware of in houses here and he said, "I've never heard of that! Maybe deep in the desert, but not in the city." I asked him if he'd ever seen one. "Well, just one tiny one about the size of a thumbnail that I thought looked almost cute." Where was it? "Oh, right outside my front door." Hmm, maybe there is something to beware of.

Another encounter with these critters was at a meeting in Dubai recently. I walked outside the church and overheard a young teenager say, "I don't want to let it go yet. I want to show it to a few more people." Then, turning to me he asked, "Hey, wanna see a scorpion?" Sure! So I went over and peered over his shoulder and sure enough, a good sized scorpion was being held captive in its "secure" cell: a Dixie cup.

"Wow, where did you get that?" I asked.

"Oh, I scooped it up inside the church!" Yep, definitely something to beware of.

Later that week I asked an Arab neighbor of mine if he'd ever seen a scorpion. My thought was, oh, he'll say no and put to rest any concern. The answer? A very affirmative nod of the head. Was it a big one? A stronger nod of the head. Where was it? "In my house!" Something to beware of? Most definitely.

I guess I've got to put my concern into perspective, though. Another friend tells the story of how he saw a young man in a rural village pick up a scorpion, place it on his head, and put a baseball cap over it. The secret? They won't sting anything they're sitting on. Nice tip, but you still won't catch me wearing a live scorpion on my head. Life is different here, and that's just another Monday in the Middle East.

April 25, 2005 – All Creatures of the Earth, Part 3

I've seen from the weather reports that tornadoes are hitting the States this time of year. Well, we haven't seen any "naders" here, but it's been raining cats and dogs since December. Normally, that would mean a flood on par with Noah's deluge, but in this sense, I mean that we have cats and dogs all over the place!

Granted, I know a city like Cairo has enough stray dogs to organize the Cairo Cacophonic Orchestra, but the few howlers here are just as annoying. A few days after we moved in, our Pakistani neighbors went to the States for a month. Come to find out, they fed a stray dog daily, so when they were gone it was more than just unhappy, it was hungry like the wolves.

This rotten mutt succeeded in waking everyone in the family night after night. I decided to do something about it, so I laid out some clothes by my bed so that when he bellered just six feet from my bedroom window, I could jump up and make chase.

Sure enough, that night it got the chase of its life. I ran out after the beast (yes, I remembered my clothes), and saw that he was really scared and my plan was working. "I'll teach that thing a lesson," I thought, so I ran two more blocks down the street to make sure he knew never to return!

Plan B. When he came back the next night (I can almost hear your laughter at my presumption) I took a different tack. I took off my belt and walked outside the house cracking it on my hands. The dog got the hint and yelped past me to escape a beating. It was yelping so pathetically that I myself had to run in the house because I didn't want the neighbors to think I was whipping the poor thing mercilessly. Honest, I didn't touch it!

I mentioned my troubles to my landlord, though. His response? "We could shoot it!" I can see it now; someone asks, "How did you get a *bullet-hole* in your truck?"

Dogs.

Life is different here, and that's just another Monday in the Middle East.

Next week, "Here kitty, kitty."

May 2, 2005 – All Creatures of the Earth, The Final Act

I'm amazed again and again at the efficiency of some things here in the Middle East. For instance, when I think of a dumpster in the U.S., I think of a green square box on wheels with plastic lids that swing over the top. Those go hand in hand with the "old style" trucks that empty the dumpsters into the back of the truck.

Here in the Middle East you can picture a simple steel box with no wheels. Watching the workers empty one of these dumpsters is a picture of simplicity. Four men simply tip the box over to reveal that it is not only open at the top, but it is open at the bottom, too. In other words, there are four square walls with all the trash on the ground, and the men simply scoop up the waste with shovels and pitch forks, and toss it into the same compacting trucks used in the States.

Obviously, this sort of system can generate a robust cloud of flies, so I usually give the bags of trash my best Perseus heave into the box from 10 to 20 feet back. The flying missles can come as quite a surprise to the stray cats scavenging last night's scraps of chicken. Imagine the kitty cat dialogue over a chunk of shish kabob, "Ahh, sweet nectar of life! Manna from heaven!" Everything's kosher until one of the cats hears the faint flutter and whisp of a grocery bag streaming through the air, "Incoming! Head for the hills!" Invariably, when one bag drops into the box I see three to four times as many cats screech into the air like I'd just launched a grenade! See, it *IS* raining cats!

The courage of those same familiar felines has outgrown the trash bin, though. One day when we hadn't thrown out the finest beef in the house, these marauders decided to work as a team to get the best pickin's of our kitchen. This plan was better than the Herodians with the Pharisees, and it almost worked. Out of nowhere I heard my wife scream from our bedroom because there was a cat in the house! Her scream sent it back out the balcony door, but she spun around only to find another one racing at her feet from the other direction! "Team work! We'll get that steak yet!"

Life is different here, and that's . . . just another Monday in the Middle East.

Flashback!
April 19, 1999 – Bombs or Chicken?
What's Your Pleasure?

Back in the U.S. I treated one of my friends to a nice Middle Eastern meal at *The Nile* restaurant in the small town of Anderson, Indiana. This was his first taste of the delicacies of ground garbanzo-bean patties deep-fried to make *falafel* sandwiches. It was his first sampling of the thick *tahini* sauce of crushed sesame seeds. My mouth waters just thinking of it!

I was actually a bit surprised, though, when he asked me bluntly, "You actually like this stuff?"

"Of course!" I responded. "It's delicious!"

"My friend," he answered, "God has specially prepared your taste buds to work in the Middle East."

I still love Arab food, and my friend still struggles to even taste it. He might get some consolation, though, from the fact that this part of the Middle East has a large number of Indian residents which gives a different flavor to living abroad. One of the favorite meals for Indians to serve at their various "pot-luck" sort of gatherings is Chicken *Biryani*. I like the taste of the meal, but I must confess that eating Chicken *Biryani* has been one of my greatest struggles in attending these gatherings. I'm not sure whether my travails can be attributed to the method of preparation or the recipe itself, but I have choked or gagged on chicken bones **every** time I have eaten *Biryani* in these seven months. Sure, it tastes good, but I value my continued existence on earth! I've got a different perspective now when I am less concerned about bombs in Iraq than I am about a plate of *Biryani*. But hey, life is different here, and that's just another Monday in the Middle East.

May 9, 2005 – An Outlawed Taste

There's an important concept to understand when traveling to the Middle East, namely, certain foods and drinks are completely forbidden. The most notable among these are alcohol and pork. Honestly, I don't care a whit about alcohol, but sometimes I get a real hankering for some old fashioned hot dogs or bacon or chopped ham on a salad. Even so, my hankerings don't come near the pork addiction of a friend who has lived and worked in the Middle East for about fifteen years.

For his first five years in the region he was in Saudi Arabia where pork and alcohol are absolutely forbidden. He tells the story of how he planned his return flights to the U.S. to include a layover of 3-4 hours in Europe. Why? He would hit the ground running in a city like Amsterdam so that within about ten minutes of landing he could gorge himself on pork. It's good for him that his cravings weren't for alcohol!

Most other countries in the Middle East allow pork for foreigners, but the pigs have their own "speakeasy" section of the grocery store. That's right, there's a separate room for anything and everything "porkish." Either that or they've got a separate, attached store with an entrance labeled in no obscure manner "Not for Muslims!" What's interesting is the contraband sold by these hog bootleggers. Of course you'll find bacon, ham, and hot dogs, but would you ever think that Miss Piggy is in jell-O? Me neither. How about Bacos? Me too, but the ingredients clearly state that Bacos contain no animal products. I'm guessing that Betty Crocker got her mix of soybean oil and sugar right because the taste itself has relegated Bacos to the swine underworld.

I recently had a Muslim friend ask me if I eat pork, so I precariously explained that I eat pork in America, but I never bring it into our house because I don't want to offend visitors like him. He further asked if the taste was good, and I said I loved it. I'd better be careful, though, especially with Bacos in the house. My friend just might get a whiff and develop a hankering for a forbidden taste.

Look out! Life is different here, and that's just another Monday in the Middle East.

Flashback!
May 3, 1999 – Dreaming of a White Christmas!

Well, it's getting hotter here in Bahrain. It's been an interesting phenomenon for me to sense a certain desire for snow and ice at this time of year. One would think that this desire for winter would come, well, at winter time, but instead it has come at the beginning of summer. In putting the pieces together, we've come to a reasonable explanation. Normally at this time of year in the U.S., winter is completely over. Since we are basking in the Bahrain sun now, this time of year means we've *missed it* completely, hence the desire for winter.

As for the heat, we just had our first day over 100 degrees this week and we can expect it to tip 100 every day from now until the end of September. If this were a city in the U.S., there would be heat warnings for at least 160 days of the year. Here are some things we've found interesting regarding heat. You know it's hot when . . .

- Laundry hanging on an outdoor line dries faster than in a drying machine.
- Cassette tapes carelessly left in a car melt.
- Even the cold water faucet puts out scalding water during the day.
- Walking outside makes the soles of your shoes sticky.
- The sea temperatures are in the mid to upper 90's.
- The hot water heater isn't needed for seven months of the year.

- It is easier to drink your DQ Blizzard than use the spoon!

While the Midwest is still having lows in the 30's and 40's, I am sure you will agree that life is different here. That's just another Monday in the Middle East.

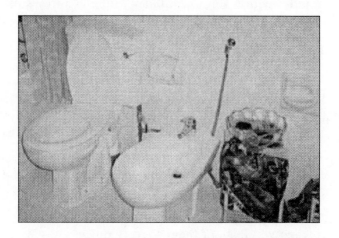

May 16, 2005 – Toilet Training in Less than an Hour
Caution: Hazardous waste ahead! Proceed at your own risk!

We had just arrived in Cyprus after a long flight with three young friends who had previously only been in the Middle East and India. Here was their first visit to Europe and their first taste of the West. I expected they would be full of questions about the cultural differences they were observing, so when they pulled me aside to ask a question privately, the only surprise was the question. With a clear sense of urgency they begged, "David, you've got to explain to us how toilet paper works!"

So there I was giving critical survival training to these 18-20 year-old guys. What an interesting clash of cultures. But would *you* need the same survival training visiting the Middle East? Fear not! Your certified toilet trainer is here!

Let's start off with your standard toilet that we're all familiar with in the States. Many bathrooms here come equipped with the toilet paper dispenser in the wall, but don't assume you'll have the paper to complete the paperwork. Better bring your own if it's that important to you.

If you don't have the toilet with TP setup, you might have a toilet with a European bidet which is a low sink for washing the nether-regions. Not much explanation needed there. Simply turn on the water and *voila*! You've got your French TP substitute.

Now we move to the Middle Eastern toilet styles. Ever wonder why Arabs always shake hands with the right hand and never, ever eat with the left hand? In the absence of toilet paper, a good old water hose from the wall will suffice. Just keep repeating, "Balance – coordination," and you'll do fine.

Next, let's fly on over to Egypt where you'll be mystified at more than just the pyramids, wondering, "Why is that metal tube pointing straight up in the middle of the toilet?" Stay seated when you flush or the discovery process might necessitate a dry set of clothes. Either that or you can "flush and dash" out of the stall before the mandatory rinse gets you.

Now on to the Gulf where we find, in Arab terms, the "Arab toilet." In expatriate circles it is affectionately known as the "squatty potty" which I can only describe as a porcelain hole in the ground that flushes. Dressed in Arab "dresses" I'm sure there would be no difficulty using one of these, but try it in binding blue jeans and you'll be wondering how in the world to maintain your balance and your cleanliness.

Finally, number one in the hall of shame is offensive to the eyes and nose. If you step into a bathroom and it smells like each stall is packed with dirty diapers, you're close to the mark in your assumption. Cause: In some countries the sewage system simply won't handle toilet paper, but the trash basket beside the toilet will!

If you're really fortunate, you'll have the option package and your house or hotel room will come equipped with everything. I think the contractors figure, "We might as well cover all the bases because we never know who's gonna need what."

Even bathroom life is different here, and that's just another Monday in the Middle East.

May 23, 2005 – Ancient Arab Secret, Huh?

Last week you got more than you ever bargained for about Arab toilets, but the wonders just go on and on. The cat is out of the bag and now you know the ancient Arab secret of clean floors. "How's that?" you ask. Again, the efficiency of some things here really amazes me, and one of those things just happens to be spic-n-span bathroom floors.

Think for a minute about all the mopping contraptions you've seen (and probably wasted money on). The old standard mop alone won't cut it, so you buy a clumsy bucket with a wringer that tips over way too easily so that the mess is more than it's worth. Or maybe yours is a simple floor, so you use a sponge mop with a wringer on the handle. Great, but you've still got to replace the mop head about every week to keep a clean floor. Simpler is often better. So, how can you put a multi-million dollar mopping industry down the drain? Here's a simple recipe:

Ingredients:
- 1 Arab bathroom hose
- 126 hard tiles (yes, I counted them)
- 1 working drain
- 1 squeegee on a stick
- Liquid disinfectant (Want to be reminded of a fruity snack? Choose orange or lemon scent. Yum. Prefer the natural smell? Stick with the Country Scent.)

To clean, simply spray floor with hose, then slosh disinfectant all over the place. Next, squeegee solution toward drain. Bingo! Bedrooms, bathrooms, kitchens – no matter. Just slide the furniture out and all the rooms can be cleaned this way.

The biggest hang-up is timing this simple procedure, and it doesn't seem the custodians here have quite mastered the skill. Picture a big mall with loads of Arab men in their white, floor-length garments. The unsuspecting victims walk innocently into a restroom only to find themselves swinging their hands wildly through the air trying to keep their balance as they slide the first few feet through the door! By the third or fourth man in the group, they've begun to tiptoe carefully across these glacé floors with arms out, ready to grab anything or anyone stable enough to keep them on their feet.

There's got to be a way for Wham-o to market this idea as year-round Slip'n Slide entertainment! At the very least, it could add some highlights to America's Funniest Home Videos. Oh, wait. This isn't America. It's just another Monday in the Middle East.

Flashback!
May 31, 1999 – Excuse Me, Please Pass the Gold Bond
It is customary in the Middle East to remove your shoes when entering a house or meeting room. Though farm boys are familiar with leaving soiled boots outside the door, I'm sure you'd have a hard time persuading a bunch of Midwestern high-school students to leave their $150 Nike shoes sitting at the door, but here, it's common practice. Some places provide little wooden cubby holes to give some order to the system, but most places just expect shoes to be left on the ground outside the door. Scores of shoes at the door of a mosque, church, or temple is a sure sign there is a rousing meeting in process. It helps that there is a sort of mutual respect that

people don't take other people's shoes, well, at least not intentionally. People have been known to walk a mile in someone else's shoes (literally!) before realizing the error.

At our church youth building the steps lead directly to the door, so there simply is no place to leave shoes outside the door. The seventy students in the youth group, then, take the liberty of leaving their shoes just *inside* the door, making an interesting and odiferous obstacle course to traverse just to get inside. Of course, high-school students are affected by 100+ degree weather as anyone else would be which gives the room a not-so-mild odor. Because of this I wasn't surprised by the suggestion of some student leaders to name the youth building "The Stable," inspired by its unique pastoral odor. Maybe some of them are farm boys after all! Take a deep breath of fresh air and say with me, life is different here, and that's just another Monday in the Middle East.

May 30, 2005 –
Einstein and Speedometers, It's All Relative

Like any high school physics lover, I wanted to test out what I was learning, so I made my own hovercraft, spy radio receiver, and other gadgets, and even tried to make my own laser. As far as the spy radio receiver, I have to send my apologies to my sister because I destroyed her radio in order to spy on her telephone conversations. Oops.

Hey, I even thought through how to test Einstein's theories. Didn't he propose that as you approach the speed of light, time approaches zero? In other words, the faster you go, everything slows down almost like you've stopped. Teenage wisdom tells you the same. After all, look on the speedometer and what do you see? The needle goes to 100, 110, 120, then what? Zero!

For all of you teenagers who really want to try this out, this is the place. The national speed limit just went up to 165.

Well, that's at least in kilometers per hour, but it's still a fast 100 miles per hour. Of course, just like in the States, people rarely drive the posted speed limit but usually add at least 10-15%. So you can assume people are really driving about 110-115 mph or more.

Before you buy your plane ticket, I should mention a slight hitch. Every car is required to have some sort of bell installed that rings constantly when traveling over 75 mph, the previous national speed limit. I'm not exactly sure what to call it, but I think an appropriate name is "annoy-o-meter." And really, that's the point, isn't it? The "Ding! Ding! Ding!" doesn't mean you've got the right answer. It means you're a speeder who has a high tolerance for environmental stress. You should apply to NASA.

So go ahead! Try your Einstein experiment! On the other hand, you'll be strengthening your ability to tune out unwanted warning noises. Maybe that ability will extend to police sirens, too.

And if he finds that your "annoy-o-meter" has been disabled, be prepared for a hefty fine. Then again, will he know without personally driving your car over 75 mph? Life is different here, and that's just another Monday in the Middle East.

Flashback!
May 24, 1999 – The Hazards of Everyday Life

Bzzzzzz. Slap! Bzzzzz. Slap! I suppose back home this is becoming quite a familiar sound about this time of year, but one of the unexpected blessings of Bahrain is few mosquitoes. The mosquitoes they do have here are so tiny, they don't compare to the blood-sucking vultures of Wisconsin.

Yes, it certainly is nice to leave windows and doors open without concern over those pesky little creatures, but it seems we've got a deadly representative of everyplace else in the animal kingdom. No swatting mosquitoes, but we might have to fend off the occasional black widow spider or the flesh-eating camel spider, but who can't tolerate that? So you might encounter a venomous scorpion curled up for a nap in your shoe, so what? Okay, we've got sea snakes, sharks, and stinging jellyfish, too. Yes, yes, we've got eight other venomous fish with deadly poison, and a few brands of barracuda, but the important thing is we don't have mosquitoes! It's one way life is different here, and that's just another Monday in the Middle East.

June 6, 2005 – It's in the Book!

OK, I have to admit that I misled you a bit last week. If you pull an "Einstein" stunt and speed along the roadway, you won't see the colorful bubbles of a police car behind you. Instead of police with radar guns, you'll notice little radar-equipped boxes positioned along the highway that will take a handsome picture of your license plate if you speed. If you like, you can even get your picture framed when you register your car and pay all of the previous year's speeding tickets at once.

It kind of makes me wonder whether speeding is a safety issue or whether the government needs an extra source of income. My car won't reach the speed limit, but I figure, hey, it's a box for pictures so I should smile and say "CHEESE" when I pass the boxes. Maybe it will brighten some pencil pusher's day when he sees some American's cheeks flapping in the wind. It'll be my version of "crying to the officer" to get out of a ticket.

My wife used a different method of getting out of a ticket, though. The first time she pulled into the full-service gas station she didn't know where the lever was to open the tank. Well, the friendly attendant helped out by pushing every button in the car until he finally found the release.

Unbeknownst to my wife, the attendant switched on the fog lights, which are illegal to use here (a bit peculiar in itself). Subsequently, she was later pulled over and the policeman asked for her license. She handed over her American driving license, but he said, "No, this isn't good enough. You need an International License." My wife reached over to our glove box and pulled out the trusty travel guide we purchased when we arrived and protested, "This says I can drive with my American license. It's in the book!"

Well, the police officer's English wasn't strong enough to read the American license, so he certainly wasn't going to stand there and read a book! Nonetheless, he warned her to keep the fog lights off and sent her on her way.

So if you're ever traveling abroad and you need some excuse for a traffic violation or cultural blooper, "It's in the book!" Life is different here, and that's just another Monday in the Middle East.

June 13, 2005 – Hot Is Cold, Cold Is Hot

Well, we've definitely turned the corner. Maybe speed doesn't actually approach zero after 120 mph, but we are living proof that when the thermometer reaches a certain point, cold becomes hot and hot becomes cold. We've gone all the way around the dial.

Our city has seen about six weeks of daily high temperatures over 100 degrees, and our daily highs for the past couple of weeks have been in the 110's. Still, how does that make hot become cold and cold become hot? Let me give you an idea of the plumbing here.

There is no city water tower to generate water pressure, so every house has a large reservoir on its flat roof to generate pressure. This tank of a couple hundred gallons tends to heat up a bit in the intense sun until the water reaches 120 degrees or more, and it feeds the water for the whole house. In other words, all the water coming to the house is over 120 degrees which doesn't make anything near a cool shower.

Fortunately, water heater bills disappear, but how do we get cool water? Well, do you remember the story about the water heaters? Each room with water facilities has its own 10 gallon electric water heater. Now here's where a paradigm shift is required. Those hot water heaters are indoors out of the hot sun, so if the heater switch is off, the water in the heater is only 105-110 degrees. Ahh, regular (albeit warm) bath water!

So if I want a relatively cool shower, I turn on just the hot. If I want a warm shower, I mix the hot with a touch of cold. If I want a hot shower, I use just the cold.

I can barely keep that straight myself, but trying to explain it to my three-year-old daughter is a real trick! "OK, from now on the 'hot' is cold and the 'cold' is hot. In about four months, the 'cold' will be cold and the 'hot' will be hot. The important thing is, don't turn on the 'hot' unless the 'hot' is cold, OK?"

"OK, Daddy!" [Translation: "Whatever you strange grown-ups say!"]

Life is different here, and that's just another Monday in the Middle East.

June 20, 2005 – Nothing Like Open Air

Back in the States I usually spend summer weekends enjoying the outdoors by camping, fishing, and hiking, or whatever. I've noticed people really enjoy the open air here, too, but it might not be by camping or rock climbing. Rather, it is by "wadi bashing" and "dune bashing." Wadis are beautiful stream beds between mountains that are the only place in the Gulf that can boast natural greenery year-round. Dunes are self-explanatory. Bashing is the process of bumping and jostling a four wheel drive vehicle through them until you find a good place to throw out some plastic mats for a picnic. It's not quite Big Sky Montana, but it's a nice Arab past time and not a bad way to spend an afternoon.

On the other hand, I've seen a new perspective on life in the open air. There's a house being constructed adjacent to ours which has introduced novel ways of thinking about the construction business. Virtually all of the workers have moved here from Afghanistan or Pakistan and live on-site for the 12 months of the project. Jumping the border for a construction job is surprising enough, but here "on-site" doesn't mean a local hotel. It really means ON SITE which makes for a very short morning commute.

Now, a few of the guys built a shanty in the back corner of the construction site where I'm guessing they have all the comforts of home like lights and a toilet. On the other hand, a few of the other workers simply sleep on cots under the deep blue sky. I'll have to say that one of those gentlemen is pretty creative, though. Just because he is sleeping under the wild blue yonder doesn't mean he can't enjoy some of those comforts of home. He used some spare lumber to construct supports and a crossbeam for his very own . . . ceiling fan. Yep, that whirring sound is a sure sign of cool comfort under the stars. Quite an inspiring natural setting, don't you think?

Who cares about whether a falling tree makes a noise if no one hears it. Is it really a ceiling fan without a ceiling? Now there's a question to keep you lying awake at night! Life is different here, and that's just another Monday in the Middle East.

June 27, 2005 – Not Quite Butterfly Kisses

In high school I encountered my first introduction to innocent signs of affection in other cultures. A simple short story told of how a young boy in Africa held hands with his same-sex friend as they walked through town. Now, let me put it this way: you wouldn't catch me dead walking through town holding hands with one of my high school wrestling/hockey/hunting buddies! But life is different here and . . . .

Some years ago, though, my wife and I were walking with an Afghan friend here in the Middle East. She was walking behind us, so she got to see how my friend reached out and took my hand as we walked through the blazing heat and humidity, and she could barely contain her snickering! Back in good old Fond du Lac, Wisconsin, that would be just a bit uncommon to say the least. Here I am in a Middle Eastern country that forbids me from holding my wife's hand, but it's no problem for my same-sex friend to reach out his sweaty palm for our little jaunt through the winding streets of Bahrain.

Well, the fun doesn't stop there! Not long after that hand-holding incident, a Bahraini friend taught me another local custom, but some written instructions might have helped. I'd observed that men give each other kisses on the cheeks when they meet each other. Kisses on both sides means you're a good friend, twice on both sides means you're a really good friend, and three times on each side means you can take a joke. Read carefully, though: a cheek kiss DOES NOT mean you use your lips! I hadn't observed quite closely enough, so I applied my lips to the scruffy beard of my Bahraini friend and had another awkward moment to wade through. No, no, a "kiss" just means put your cheek next to his and make a kissing sound with your lips. Feign friendly affection even if you don't touch him.

After observing the local custom here in Oman, again I uttered those famous last words, "I won't be caught dead . . . ." The idea of nose kisses isn't my thing, but when I shook a friend's hand and he pulled me close and touched his nose to mine, I didn't really have a choice. I think he got the idea it isn't my thing, though. You know that look a person has as the roller coaster hits the top and begins its dive into the fastest twisting and turning permitted by anatomy? I think that look on my face told all because my friend commented in Arabic, "I think this is your first time for that, right?" You could say that.

Now, though, the nose touch with a kissing sound is becoming second nature. Weird? Oh yeah, really weird when I think about it from an American perspective.

So if you ever experience Middle Eastern affection, consider it an honor that you are a close and trusted friend. Yeah, life is different here, and that's just another Monday in the Middle East.

Flashback!
April 27, 1999 – The Marching Faithful

The U.S. State Department has all sorts of warnings available for Americans traveling abroad. If situations get tense in a particular country, they'll issue a warning that says something like, "American citizens are advised to avoid crowded areas such as shopping areas, malls, etc." I suppose in wiser days I might have heeded that advice, but back in January I couldn't resist checking something out personally.

I was simply trying to fall asleep when I heard a sort of drum beat outside my window. I got up to find a march of thousands of Muslim men packing the streets only a block from our apartment. I went down and walked up slowly to the street to see the march of organized lines five to six feet apart to commemorate the birthday of Ali, a Muslim saint. Walking to the beat of a chanter they synchronized their movements and beat their chests together in one thunderous blast every few seconds, leaving an incredible impression of unity.

That march in January was only in one city, but another march today will be across the entire country with possibly 100,000-200,000 people involved. Today, the Shiite Muslims will celebrate the second day of *Ashoora*, a holiday to remember the martyrdom of Hussayn. This holiday's most striking feature is not just men beating their chests, but beating their backs with chains, and some even slashing themselves with razors. Now, I've had Easter celebrations that included a call to deep remorse for sin, but I can't remember any Easter that included bloodletting in the streets! Well, except the first one. Definitely, life is different here, but that's just another Monday in the Middle East.

July 4, 2005 – Circle the Wagons!

Overseas terrorism is a real threat, but honestly, you have to look at things in perspective. For instance, The World's

Most Dangerous Places says that your most likely means of death overseas is heart disease, just like in the U.S. of A. In fact, you're three times more likely to die of a lightning strike at home than you are in overseas terrorism—anywhere in the world, including Columbia, Chechnya, and Liberia. Realistically, one of the most hazardous things you can do in the Middle East is get into a car, and I tend to think that taxis have a particular edge in the realm of danger.

Here, we are blessed with buzzing taxis everywhere, careening wildly around corners, seemingly immune to traffic laws. They keep you alert while driving, but because there are so many taxis, they offer pretty cheap transportation. Why are there so many? Well, registering a taxi is cheaper than registering a private vehicle, so a lot of people register their private vehicles as taxis, paint them orange and white, and make a few bucks while driving around town.

Yesterday, I couldn't get a taxi for the life of me. I carried my three-year-old daughter nearly a mile and still, no taxi. Loads of the them drove by, but they wouldn't stop. Finally, a man stopped in his own private vehicle. Oh, it's my good friend Tariq from Egypt whom I've never seen before and will never see again. Hey, anyone offering help is a good friend in those circumstances! Tariq gave us a quick ride to the city center in his Mercedes Benz so I could catch a real taxi.

As we got out, behold! A taxi had just dropped someone off, so I walked over and told the driver I was headed to the neighboring city over the border. He said that was no good, but his current passenger, whom I'll call, Mr. Afghan protested, "No, no, it's OK, let him in!" What a kind gesture from Mr. Afghan! Not only that, but when we drove to the second taxi stand to catch a ride across the border, he even carried my bag while I carried my daughter and we crammed into a nearly full taxi and got on our way. Hey, five smelly, sweaty men and one little girl packed into a compact car works, especially when it costs me a grand total of $1 to get home!

So a taxi really can be a home for hospitality. It can even be a home! Groups of homeless taxi drivers corral their taxis into a circle at the edge of the desert, pull out mattresses from their trunks, and have a regular nightly camp-out. You could even say that's the modern upgrade to "Circle the wagons!" but I don't think cabbies in the urban jungles of America would get much sleep. America is too dangerous, but not here where life is different, and that's just another Monday in the Middle East.

Flashback!
June 7, 1999 – Blown Away

Of course, with everything that is going on with Yugoslavia and Kosovo right now, Iraq seems to be small beans. However, here in Bahrain, Iraq is still a big issue. In fact, we've been hit twice here just this year! No, no, we weren't hit by bombs, but rather, sandstorms.

The Middle East is famous for storms that sandblast everything in sight. They arrive in minutes, literally, and they can leave in just as short of time. A foreigner I heard of used a video recorder to capture the dusty wall of a sandstorm moving across the desert toward his town. Before your eyes, the video shows the buildings of the town quickly disappearing into blackness. With that amount of dust blowing around, I'd be willing to venture that this video was the last one that camera ever recorded!

Meteorologists tell us that the two major sandstorms that clouded our skies this year picked up their loads of sand and grit in the deserts of Iraq and Syria and dumped them on us over 1,000 miles away with a force greater than an atomic bomb. Yesterday's storm not only reduced visibility like a dense fog, but it forced us to nix the air conditioner which was pumping in more dust than air! What is that proverb? If you wash your car, it's guaranteed to rain? Here, if you wash your car, you're guaranteed a sandstorm. And grab the Windex on the way out the door; just like with Wisconsin snow, you'll need to clean your windows before leaving the scene of the grime. Life is same-same, but different here, and that's just another Monday in the Middle East.

July 11, 2005 – The Chase of the Storm Chaser!

I love storms. They show me how powerful God is and how tiny I am. No matter how terrified I might get in the middle of one, I'm thrilled when the next one comes along. However, most days now in the Middle East are like today — sunny, clear, and about 114 degrees.

So today was a great day to enjoy a free trial membership at the Hilton Hotel sports club. This place is like paradise, and I had a wonderful day of swimming with my family. About 4 p.m., though, I heard what sounded like strong thunder and my life-guarding instincts warned me to get the kids out of the pool. Lightning, though? I could see a bit of dust in the air, but that was it. I guess I could envision dust particles rubbing together to generate static electricity just like rain, but on a nice day like today it just didn't make sense.

About three minutes later, we were out of the pool and I saw it coming! Looking over the trees I could see a 1000-foot-high red sand cloud moving our way. I was so impressed that I called my kids over to show them, and I explained that in about five minutes, we were going to have sand dumped all over us. Well, it didn't take five minutes—it took about 30 seconds! Only five minutes after I'd first heard the thunder, I looked up toward the tops of the palm trees swaying calmly about 100 feet away. In one violent blast, this sand cloud came hurtling over the trees! Leaves and debris blew in a straight line from the tops of those trees right to my face. I was awe-struck at the force of this storm, but I couldn't stand there for long! All three of my kids were instantly screaming in terror at the table umbrellas, seat cushions, and tree branches flying over the pool. I've seen greater wind speeds before, but I have never experienced such a fast moving storm.

The scarves that the Bedu men and women of the desert wear might seem strange to us, but I learned their value first-hand today. The Bedu understand that storms like this one come on in minutes, so they always need to be ready to pull their head scarves over their eyes, nose, and mouth simply to breathe. Today, I saw this storm blast in from a calm day straight into my eyes in just seconds. Life IS different here, and that's just another Monday in the Middle East.

Flashback!
June 28, 1999 – Pest Control

It seems that loitering can be a problem in any city. I suppose people just sitting anyplace along the street can change the appearance of a city, and that's just the argument I've been reading in news about loitering laws back home. Here in Manama, Bahrain, we still have a lot of loitering, but it isn't because of a lack of effort to deter it. What's the method of choice for deterrence? It isn't a law or signs or even police writing out tickets, but just your basic metal spikes bolted into the base of storefront window sills all along busy streets. Talk about your city appearance!

Naturally, one would want to deter such things as burglary, though, and a similar approach is used to keep thieves at bay. Here in Bahrain, a law requires each property to have a surrounding wall whether knee high or ten feet high. Many residents here have taken things a bit further by installing various sorts of spikes to keep more athletically gifted thieves from scaling the top. The cheapest approach is to pour a thin layer of concrete atop the wall, then break glass soda bottles and tip the neck upside down into the concrete. I'm quite sure that if you tried that in the U.S., you'd be sued instantly by the thief who cut himself while trying to rob your house. Maybe Bahrain isn't such a land of blessing for lawyers.

Any way you look at it, you won't see much loitering on the spiked window sills of Manama, and I doubt too many thieves are interested in high jumping these razor-topped walls. All that considered, where's the concept of a friendly-looking business? Life is different here, and that's just another Monday in the Middle East.

July 18, 2005 – Out of the Box Pest Control

I'm reading a book about an Arabian traveler named Wilfred Thesiger. He is famous for being the only European to cross the Rub al Khali (Empty Quarter) twice by camel. Now this is no picnic in the park even to do it once, but to do it twice is amazing. This section of the Arabian desert is called the Empty Quarter for good reason; nothing lives there! Picture half a million square miles of sand dunes up to 800 feet deep with no living creatures. No birds, no insects, no animals except, as Thesiger discovered, a locust breeding ground every time it rains.

He describes seeing so many locusts swarm a tree that the boughs themselves sheared off under the sheer weight of hundreds of thousands of these little insects. He notes that they are as numerous as snowflakes in a blizzard when they swarm, blocking out nearly every glimmer of light in the sky. They can strip bare a whole field of green vegetation in just hours. Think of a cloud of insects miles long and hundreds of yards deep . . . John the Baptist could make one serious locust sandwich!

I stirred up my own insect swarm the other day. I've mentioned before that the previous residents of our apartment suffered through a gas treatment without masks all on account of winged termites in a door frame. Yep, the diesel fuel did the trick for a while, but I noticed the same visitors on the same door eating the same lunch recently.

So, I discovered another method of extermination that is a bit more environmentally friendly, although not so "permanent." Thinking a bit outside the box, I gave them a ride on the Hoover express. I found that our trusty vacuum cleaner quite handily transports these swarming wood buzzards to a cushy new air bag bed deep in its belly. In fact, it seemed a bit like sport for my son and me—he'd bang on the door frame with the hammer, and I'd welcome them to their new home.

This plan was working well until I discovered the power of swarming "anythings." I decided that in order to really get them out, I'd need to take off that part of the door frame. Trust me, I opened more than a Pandora's Box! Literally thousands and thousands of termites poured out into my bedroom, leaving me and my son standing in a cloud of them wondering what's next. Praise the Lord for ceiling fans! At full speed, the fan knocked them down to the floor pretty effectively, but I had to go in and vacuum hundreds of them off the floor about every five to ten minutes . . . for the next six hours!

It's no wonder historians say the Middle East is the cradle of civilization. It has been and still is home to every creeping and swarming thing since Creation! Life is different here, and that's just another Monday in the Middle East.

Flashback!
June 14, 1999 – The Forest for the Trees

In places like New York or Chicago, you'd pay a fortune to have an inner-city apartment with a forest view. Well, our fourth floor apartment boasts an amazing forest view in the capital city of Manama. The forest doesn't consist of Appalachian hardwoods or Minnesota pines, but of radio antennas, television antennas, and the associated satellite dishes. Yeah, the scenery of the rooftops is sorely lacking, but even outside the city, Bahrain doesn't have the incredible vistas of Niagara Falls by any means. The desert here doesn't so much remind me of a soft sandy beach as it does a sun-baked gravel road. In fact, the Sheikh of the country imported sand from Italy to complete his own private beach! I'll have to concede that it is a beautiful beach, but come on now, importing sand to the Middle East?

This made us all the more eager to take full advantage of our recent visit to the United Arab Emirates where most of the country towers with beautiful red sand dunes of 500-700 feet high. Seeing as how we'd missed the fun of making snow angels this past winter, we took it upon ourselves to initiate a new tradition of making sand angels in the desert. Even our American host thought this was a bit peculiar, but for us it was a Kodak moment to contrast with the bleak forest view from our Bahraini apartment. You see, life is different here, and life is different there, but it's still just another Monday in the Middle East.

July 25, 2005 – Spinning "Fives"

I love sports, but I especially love the Packers. When I'm back in the States watching football with the family, I celebrate loudly with vigor. At each Packer touchdown I do my own Lambeau Leap across the living room crushing my brother-in-law and whomever else is daring enough to sit on the sofa. I guess you could say I really get into the game.

They love football here, too, but it's "football" with a black and white checkered ball. Funny thing, it's really played with the feet! Soccer is a huge hit and any given afternoon around 5:30 just before sundown you're bound to see a pick-up game on any block.

Their enthusiasm doesn't stop with their own abilities to play soccer, though. A number of nights I've been outside and I hear the telltale signs of a major victory of someone's favorite team. The raucous squealing of tires might sound like twenty different car accidents happening all across town, but it's really only about a hundred high school boys racing around town burning rubber to show their joy. I guess they think if they have enough cars doing it simultaneously in different places, they're less likely to get caught!

Though I've never found proof in books, I think there really must be a link in the Arab mind between soccer and peeling rubber, but that link is oddly absent in my mind.

69

There's even a name for this past-time: spinning "fives." We might call it "spinning donuts" or "spinning cookies," but the resulting rubber circles on the pavement resemble the Arabic numeral for five: ٥.

So even though I may not have a mental link between squealing tires and sports victory, I do have a peculiar link between squealing tires and delicious desserts. Kinda makes you wonder, who's the strange one here?

Ask me that same question on September 11 as I listen to the Packers' opening game on the Internet and make my first Lambeau Leap of the year onto an empty sofa. You just might have your answer! Life is different here, and that's just another Monday in the Middle East.

August 1, 2005 – "Scram!" "Welcome back!"

An inescapable aspect of the Middle East is getting here and staying here. Getting here can mean anything from a flight next to royalty of one of the smaller sheikhdoms or it could mean holding back your surprise at goats and chickens in the cabin.

Staying here has its varying forms, too. In some countries you don't need a visa at all. It's as easy as Americans visiting Canada. In others, you need to show receipts of a certain dollar amount of hard currency that you've put into the local economy. If you buy groceries and show the receipts, you can renew your tourist visa and stay another month.

In most Middle Eastern countries, though, you receive a one-month non-renewable tourist visa with a one-month grace period. In laymen's terms, you're free to stay two months, but then, "Scram, pal!"

The funny thing about the forceful deadline of 60 days is the system to get around it. Every 60 days we drive to the border past the intimidating government signs that say "No Photographs!" Then the friendly people at the window say, "Scram pal!" (Not an exact translation). About half an hour later when we return from the checkpoint of the neighboring country with our two new passport stamps, the same gentleman says, "Welcome back!"

If anyone thinks using a tourist visa like this is surreptitiously slipping past the government, you've got another thing coming. Not only did I get my first-ever retinal scan on one of these "visa runs," but this last time I was surprised by a more personal welcome. I drove my borrowed vehicle up to check out of the U.A.E., and before I even said hello to the officer he said, "You're David, right?" Whoa, I don't even own this car, yet they connected my name and passport number to this car from my last sneaky visa run! "Pretty slick," I thought as I drove away wondering how many camera eyes were on me. "If I knew you were comin', I'd have baked a cake . . . ." I'll put my order in now for a thick chocolate one with wavy chocolate frosting on top. Hey, you know I'll be back in 60 days; you might as well make it to order!

Life is different here, and that's another Monday in the Middle East.

Flashback!
August 2, 1999 – The Rocky Road to Mecca

At some point in their lives most Muslims perform the requisite hajj, or pilgrimage to Mecca, with its associated rites. This pilgrimage to Islam's two holiest cities of Mecca and Medina is to be completed once in a person's lifetime if financially feasible. A friend here in Bahrain performed the hajj this past year and he came back with a humorous story. At one point in the hajj, each participant is to pick up seven pebbles to throw at a particular stone pillar. It is important to note that this pillar represents Satan, so throwing these stones is a personal witness against evil. Consequently, the stones are to be thrown with some vehemence, considering the one they are throwing them at. When Islam began in the seventh century only a scant few people performed the hajj, but today one and a half million people must throw seven stones at this one pillar! Obviously, one and a half million people could not get as close to the monument as they might have liked so they simply threw the stones in the general direction of the pillar from wherever they were standing. Needless to say, more than a few people who were lucky enough to get close to the monument discovered how unlucky this pole position is when they experienced the force of others' "personal witness against evil." Ouch! Anyone got a band-aid? Life is different here, and that's just another Monday in the Middle East.

August 8, 2005 – Y2K All Over Again

When you think back to December of 1999, can you remember what all the furor was about? Much of the world approached the New Year ill at ease, hearing potential of modern society returning to the Dark Ages. On the whole, glitches were minor, though. For instance, one computer in my workplace showed that a girl in the preschool program was 104 years old! Even though that problem took two months to straighten out, it was still a minor issue.

There's a good reason for that smooth transition into Y2K; people took it seriously and worked feverishly to make sure things were in order. One thing Y2K taught us was to think ahead. This week, people in Saudi Arabia are experiencing the same need for preparations I experienced in Bahrain in 1999. King Fahd of Saudi Arabia died this past week and in the Middle East, that's a big deal. All radio and TV stations go into a 24-hour-a-day reading of the Koran to begin an official period of mourning. Channel 3? Mourning. Channel 7? Mourning. Channel 9? News! (About the death and mourning). Everything closes to give people an "opportunity" to mourn.

Here's my Monday in the Middle East from May 17, 1999, after the death of the ruler of Bahrain.

Continual Y2K Preparations

That is one way that I can describe life in the Middle East. All over the world millions of people are stocking food, buying generators, and cutting firewood for the disaster that the Millennium Bug could bring, but here we just have day-to-day life to get us ready. For instance, several weeks back the Emir of Bahrain died and *everything* was closed for five days. Having plans to go to a nice restaurant for dinner didn't make a difference – the restaurant was closed along with the gas stations, corner drug stores, *everything*. But it's not just mourning periods that bring about these inconveniences. We also had our water suddenly go out without warning. So much for that morning shower I'm used to. Our natural gas, too. Who needs to cook anyway? Electricity? Rolling power cuts of 2-3 hours each move across the country every day of every summer. Looks like a good time to enjoy some A/C at the malls. The Internet? We're talking worse than AOL! Trying to check email after 4:30 p.m. is a guaranteed standoff with at least 10-12 busy signals. Right now, our phone service is out for some reason so even if I could connect . . . you get the idea. The Middle East may be hit hardest by the Millennium Bug, but we'll be the best prepared! That makes life different here. That's just another Monday in the Middle East.

P.S. This column is certified Y2K compliant.

August 15, 2005 – Designer Black

One of the most striking aspects of arrival in the Arabian Gulf is the fashion of Muslim women. It might seem like a simple black covering, but trust me, there are more ways to cover Middle Eastern women than shoes in Imelda Marcos' closet! Some women prefer the simple hair shawl while others use a full body covering complete with black gloves, a separate head covering, another face covering with only eye slits, and a drop-down covering over the slits so that the world is viewed through sheer black. Fortunately for everyone, these coverings are not permitted while driving!

It is amazing to recognize the pride taken in wearing uni-color black. Some of these garments are adorned with lace edging, some with sheen designs woven in, and some with ornate beads and sequins stitched intricately to capture the eye. Even the manner of wearing them varies so that some veils are wrapped tightly around the face while others hang loosely. Some women leave their hair down under the veils and others bundle long hair high on their heads. One of our Arab friends uses the nickname "camel humps" for these mounds on account of the disproportionately tall head beneath.

Of course, in theory all of the coverings are intended to conceal the shape of a woman's body, but some women are more intentional about this concealment than others. For instance, an Arab language teacher shared the popular name of the more modern garments as *abayya franciyya*. The beginning Arabic student would recognize *abayya* as the name of the garment, but *franciyya*? Welcome to the world of Arab fashion! Apparently, the French dominate *abayya* design too, so much so that the teacher even drew a white-board picture of the tight, hip-hugging, form-fitting garments to clarify with certainty: *Abayya franciyya*!

So if you see a woman sporting "Christian" on her camel hump, assume "Dior" rather than religion. French style and French label right here in historic Arab tradition! Life is different here, and that's just another Monday in the Middle East.

August 22, 2005 – Middle East Dating Services

Last week's introduction to women's coverings here in the Middle East may have given you the impression that young men and young women are far from each other's minds, but this is far from the truth. In fact, the local dating service is just about the most ubiquitous industry in the region and it goes by such names as Nokia and Ericsson. Telephone dating is all the rage here, just like Internet dating in the U.S., but it's not just you calling me and us talking into the wee hours of the morning. No, no, no. That would be boring! Dating with a mobile phone has a much more complex and personal dynamic!

First, you've got to know someone who knows someone, if you know what I mean. (Sounds kind of like a Mafia ring, and if you lower your voice and talk quietly out the side of your mouth with an Italian accent, it works.) Then you have that someone give someone a call to meet someone someplace sometime. Usually, it's the local mall. Once you've got all the someones in place, you make the call. "Ring! Ring!" Now you know what someone looks like! You can safely sit across the food court and watch each other's simultaneous laughter at how clever you were to avoid even asking your parents' permission to meet someone. And if they ask who you're talking to, you can say, "Oh, just someone." Congratulations on your first mobile phone date!

It is quite a system, but to what avail? Would people really consider marrying someone from a simple telephone conversation? Undoubtedly!

One of my wife's friends received a "prank" call several months ago. Actually, the caller was just dialing number after number until he found a young lady who would talk to him. Then she received another call from the same young man the next day, then the next day, and so on. For several months he's been persisting with this young woman he's never met. Why? "The moment I heard your voice I fell in love with you!" Great one-liner, but I doubt it. I imagine he's thinking if he meets Mrs. Right this way, God has willed it.

And if he should find Mrs. Right, they can certainly say it was a match made in the heavens. Well, the airwaves, anyway. Life is different here, and that's just another Monday in the Middle East.

August 29, 2005 – "Oh, the Eyes!"

Yeah, no matter how you look at it, dating in the Middle East has got to be a challenge. For instance, most marriages are arranged through the parents. That means you might end up marrying Great Aunt Ethel's granddaughter whom you haven't seen since she was seven. Even so, the prospect of dating or falling in love keeps young men and women . . . engaged, shall we say.

I was rattling along with one of my friends about college life at his university in Salalah, Oman. Now, Salalah sounds like an interesting place. When it's blistering hot summer in the rest of Oman, Salalah is blooming with flowers and green plants with cool temperatures and tropical rains. Even the mountains separating Salalah from half a million square miles of desert sand turn green with lush plant life. It might seem like a tourist's tropical paradise, but the city boasts no malls—not even a supermarket. I guess people just come to enjoy the natural beauty, or beauties as my friend would have me believe.

He tells me of how boring life is in Salalah, but suddenly a wide-eyed expression comes over his face as he says, "But the women there are VERY beautiful! These women come down from the mountains to the university, and they are very, very beautiful."

Now wait a minute here. I live in a conservative area where most women wear *abayyas* (*franciyya* or otherwise) and many women wear the full face covering. Guessing that these mountain women are at least that conservative, I protest, "Don't they wear veils over their faces?"

"Yes."

"Then how do you know if they are beautiful if you can't even see their faces?"

Without a snap of hesitation my friend exclaims, "Oh, the eyes! You just look at her eyes and know she is sooooo beautiful!"

All you single ladies out there take heart! Next time you put your picture on an Internet dating service, submit only a picture of your eyes. I've got verifiable evidence that it's all a guy needs to fall in love with you. Well, then again . . . life is different here, and that's just another Monday in the Middle East.

September 5, 2005 – Behind the Veil

My friend may insist that the eyes are all that's needed to fall in love, but there's a serious problem here. Many women wear what's called a *ghashwa* which covers the face entirely so that women simply look through a dark screen of fabric. This presents a bit of a drawback for men of the Middle East in that, when meeting these women, they never know what sort of trouble they might be getting into.

For example, one of our Arab friends tells us of an exchange she witnessed at the local mall. On any given weekend, you're likely to find a bunch of college-age guys hanging out at the mall trying to gain the interest of college-age women. Well, at least that's the intent, and these fully-veiled women wearing *ghashwas* are not exempt. You might even witness a group of guys wooing a group of girls with all their might. Following and flirting seems to be the manner of approach, but note the missing information: just how old are these women? A man with a keen eye can watch a woman's gait and maybe detect high heels. If so, he can generally rule out AARP material, but otherwise, he really has no clue about how old she is.

The poor man of today's story followed two young (?) women out of the mall and started hitting on them, trying to pass along his phone number. Only then did the taller one wheel around and shout, "Shame on you! Don't you know I can tell your mother?" Turns out, it was one of his mother's close friends with her daughter. Woo becomes whoops.

On the other hand, *ghashwas* present problems for the bearer as well. Case in point, a teacher told my wife about the first time she wore a *ghashwa*. She had been annoyed that the taxi driver seemed to be watching her in the rear view mirror, hence, she pulled her thin veil over her face. Reaching her destination, she exited the taxi, paid the fare, and proceeded to walk . . . into the wrong building. I suppose partial blindness takes some getting used to.

An alternative to the *ghashwa* is the *burka* which is a metallic-looking covering hung in front of the eyebrows and mouth. Its mustache shape over a woman's lips leaves her eyes unhindered. My wife asked the same teacher if she would ever wear one of these *burkas.* "No!" came the reply sharply. "That's just for old ladies who can't see!"

My wife pressed further, "What do you mean, 'Old ladies who can't see?'"

The teacher answered, "They have to wear *burkas.* If they wear *ghashwas* they'll just run into everything!"

So I guess good vision is a prerequisite to restricting your vision. In that regard, one of those 20/20 young women sported a *ghashwa* while riding in a car with my wife and son. Wanting to instill a bit of etiquette into our son, my wife introduced them, saying, "Jonathan, this is Mrs. Basima." To that, Basima jeered, "Cheryl, he can't see me; he has no idea who I am!"

Uh-huh. Life is different here, and that's just another Monday in the Middle East.

September 12, 2005 – That Youthful Look

In meeting new people with a new language there are a few questions and answers that you need to know to get past the first few minutes. You're familiar with most of them, I am sure: What is your name? Where are you from? How long have you been here? How old are you? Are you married? Do you have any children? Where do you work?

One of those has been a lot of fun to play around with since I arrived here ten months ago. I've always looked younger than I actually am, and people tell me over and over, "Wait until you're 40 and you look like you're 30; you'll appreciate it!" That day still hasn't come. Mom always told me, "Act your age." I'm doing my best, Mom, but at this point, I want to look my age, too!

In the Middle East the common denominator for maturity of men is facial hair. In some places this concept is so clearly defined that young men aren't allowed to grow a mustache until they are married. Then, when the man has his first child, he can grow a goatee, then a full beard as he fathers more and more children.

For me, I simply haven't been blessed with the feature of strong facial hair. Many of you who know me can attest to this by my bedraggled look during many failed attempts to "look my age."

Since I don't have a beard or goatee or mustache, though, I can have some fun with my youthful look. I often challenge folks I meet by asking them how old they think I am. Virtually all the answers I get span from 17 to 25 and one guess of 32—just one year shy of the 33 years that I actually am. Everyone I ask, though, is astonished that I have four children and I've been married for nearly 10 years.

It's entirely in your hands to follow your mother's advice to act your age. I'll leave that up to you. But if you want to look your age, the moral of the story is a simple one: Never underestimate the power of a furry lip.

Life is different here, and that's just another Monday in the Middle East.

September 19, 2005 – Duct Tape Censorship

The scene is building and you can sense the romance in the air. Soft music plays in the background. A picturesque sunset colors the landscape over a mountain backdrop. Now, the handsome man wraps his arm around a lovely woman and draws her in close. Finally, he gently holds her face in his hands and . . . suddenly he's playing tennis with a business partner!

Scenes like these can turn any romance into a comedy, and there's really no way around it. In this part of the world, movies are clipped and cut to remove every trace of love scenes, and even a peck on the lips is out of the question. It's unabashed censorship and it thrives in the Middle East!

Certainly, the ACLU would have a field day with frivolous lawsuits here since the censorship doesn't stop with movies. In fact, when entering the country you will likely only have your luggage inspected if the X-ray shows any video tapes with you. Whether they are tapes of your latest family reunion or the whole Veggie Tales set, the dutiful customs official will watch each of them which can be a time-consuming review of your video collection.

Regarding mail, I've even had a magazine opened simply because it was in an opaque envelope. The note inside assured me it was "Opened for official government purposes," but I would have paid money to see their expressions when they discovered my ultra-secret, 007, CIA, MI-6, FBI manual surreptitiously entitled *Christianity Today*.

Oh, and this was especially fun. Walking through the mall, I enjoyed 70 or 80 intriguing photographs in framed displays. Many were award winning photographs of people or still-life photos giving a snapshot of history, but something was amiss. Alas! It was the black duct tape pasted over the skirt that might be too short or over the immodest bathing suit! Now there's a new one for your DUCT TAPE USES book!

Tops, though, in my censorship humor book is a purchase from a large department store in a pretty modern city. I found a stack of laminated world maps that could serve as place mats on a child's desk, so I picked one up for my son. When I got home I discovered that a country was missing! Indeed, someone had gone through all of those maps one by one with a black permanent marker to blot out the name "Israel" from every one. I think someone's got a little too much time on his hands.

Perhaps this is what Iran meant when they threatened to wipe Israel off of the map. However you look at it, life is different here, and that's just another Monday in the Middle East.

September 26, 2005 – Excited Shoppers

Just because you walk into a supermarket, you don't expect everyone to be super. Imagine walking into IGA and hearing, "Hello there! You're a super guy and we've got lots of super people to serve up some super deals! Have a super day!" No, the "super" clearly refers to the store, not the people.

Here in the Middle East, the same type of stores are called "Hypermarkets," so it's tempting to ask whether "hyper" refers to the store, like in the U.S., or does it refer to the people? Well, I haven't seen too many stores frenetically racing around the city, so I think it's safe to infer that "hyper" must refer to the people. If that is the case, these hypermarkets certainly fit the bill!

The hustle and bustle of these stores is enough to get you to check your pulse. My blood pressure goes up just walking in the door, I'm sure of it. Yesterday, I saw a worker bring out a new pallet of tomatoes and the people were on them like fruit flies. He was having trouble dumping the crates onto the stacks since shoppers were simply snatching tomatoes straight off of the pallet one by one. Hey, they're just tomatoes and everybody knows that tomatoes are only good for ketchup and spaghetti sauce [personal opinion free of charge].

That same chaotic visit, a new bin of something was placed in a center aisle. I still don't know what it was, but that misses the point; it was new! It could have been Hollywood's latest DVDs or discounted boxes of laxatives, but whatever it was, about 20 people descended on it like vultures on fresh road kill. I was tempted to dive in the pile myself, but I've been trying to cut back on my squirrel intake.

My advice would be, if you find yourself in one of these "Hypermarkets," keep some nitroglycerin pills handy just in case you get swept into the fray. When all is said and done, you'll safely carry out your tomatoes, DVDs, and laxatives with a story to tell. Life is different here, and that's just another Monday in the Middle East.

October 10, 2005 – Why Did the Camel Cross the Road?

It's not uncommon to see interesting animals while driving which is one of the reasons I enjoy getting out on the road. It doesn't matter whether I am in the Middle East or hick Indiana, I enjoy strange people and interesting scenery.

Today I had a bit of both right here in the Middle East. Driving along on the highway, you'd expect to be passing cars, but today I passed a camel. The camel wasn't equipped with turn signals, so I didn't use mine. In fact, the camel was parked in the median between the two lanes of traffic whizzing by at 60 mph. I thought it was a bit odd, but I know there are some wild roaming camels here, so I thought perhaps this was such an example. As it turns out, its ankles were lashed together loosely to keep it from running too fast, which would indicate some level of domestication.

From another perspective, the rope on the legs meant that, not only did this camel sashay half way across this dangerous road, but it meandered slowly, patiently enduring its "handcuffs"! I sure hope I'm nowhere nearby when it decides to continue its little jaunt from the median.

On the other hand, traveling in a car would be much safer for any animal rather than running across the road on their own power. Consider the following scenario. There is a strong aversion to dogs here that could even be characterized as a fear of dogs. Because of this, I didn't expect to see an Irish Wolfhound in the back of a station wagon, but that was just what I saw! As I pulled closer, I saw that the shaggy hair wasn't that of a Wolfhound at all, but instead, a floppy-eared billy goat! As I passed by the car I checked to see if the driver was smiling while his billy goat teetered back and forth trying to keep its balance with every turn and press of the brake. Nope, no special expression at all! This is normal life to him, but to me, well, life is different here, and that's just another Monday in the Middle East.

P.S. My wife (born and raised in hick Indiana) would like me to issue a disclaimer that maybe life isn't so different here; her father drove their goats around in the back of the car all the time. Like I said, interesting scenery and . . . you get the idea.

October 17, 2005 –
Camel Sale! Bring Your Own Ratchet Tie-Downs!
    I once heard a radio host in St. Paul give a new nickname to PETA (People for the Ethical Treatment of Animals).

His not-so-politically-correct nickname was People for the Eating and Tasting of Animals, and I imagine that gets the hackles up on a few listeners in the city once known as Pig's Eye. The real PETA wouldn't be any more pleased with the State of the Animal in the Middle East, either.

You never know, though. Is your friend of the Ethical Treatment stripe or of the tribe of Eating and Tasting? Consider this dandy faux pas. I sat down at a Chili's restaurant and mentioned to my friend how Chili's in the Middle East is sorely lacking in the wonderful taste of bacon. Only then did I realize that I hadn't checked if this Indian fellow had any reticence to eating ham or any meat for that matter. When I asked if he ate meat, he quickly answered, "Anything that moves!" Ahh, what a relief! A kindred spirit on the Animal Kingdom.

If that doesn't get PETA's pants in a bundle, there's plenty more ill treatment of creatures to deal with. For instance, the most reasonable transport for a newly-purchased camel is a nice pick-up (preferably without the topper). There isn't really a size requirement to the truck; a truck the size of a Chevy S-10 can haul a 1,500 lb. camel, although there's no guarantee against wheelies. You've also got to consider that you might make better time riding the camel and leaving the truck.

So how do you pack a camel that is seven feet tall at the shoulders into a tiny Toyota? Lots of brute force! At least two to three men in front are required to pull the rope that is strapped around the moaning camel's head while another five to six men go shoulder to rump with the backside of that bawling beast to shove it onto the truck.

Once it's on board, the next step is forcing it to kneel so that the legs can be bound to prevent it from standing up. That would make an interesting trip beneath the underpass, wouldn't it?

Finally, you might not think of it, so I'll say it straight out: tie the head to the center of the truck. With a neck that's 3-4 feet long, a nosy camel could easily stick his head over the drivers' side of the pickup and discover the striking reality of oncoming traffic. You know what they always say: Curiosity killed the camel.

You betcha, life is different here, and that's just another Monday in the Middle East.

October 24, 2005 –
"Lord, I'll Get It Down If You Keep It Down."

I have a faint memory of a day as a five-year-old boy begging my mom to allow me to help her wash the dishes. This must be one of those "fleeting desires of youth" the Bible talks about because to the best of my recollection, that was the last day I ever wanted to wash dishes. What is it about washing dishes that repels us so much? Did each of us drink a bottle of dishwashing repellent after that first day of eagerness? Still, they've got to be done.

Whatever the force is that pushes us from dishes, it is hard at work here in the Middle East, but here the dishwashing goes through some serious shortcuts, namely, no soap!

Sitting down for a cup of coffee at a friend's house is an interesting introduction to this. First, I am treated to a bowl of fresh dates which I smash open with only my right hand in order to extract the seed. Next, I have to wash my hands from the sticky, sugary dates, and I do this with all the other gentlemen in the room in a small bowl of water. Next, we are treated to cups of Arab coffee, after which the cups are "washed" by rinsing them in the sticky water we all just washed our hands in. Interesting.

I had an ... interesting ... cup of coffee at an Arab wedding, too, but I think my degree of tolerance for unsanitary conditions rose dramatically. The coffee tasted fine, but then I observed the dishwashing. I'll just say, it wasn't quite "up to code." A waiter walked around pouring a cup of coffee for each of us then waited for us to drink it on the spot. He then filled the cup for the man next to me and so on. After every couple of rows of people, he would pass the four cups to another man who would "wash" them with the thorough rinsing method cited above.

Excuse me? Two hundred toothless old men have put their dusty lips to this cup before me, and now I'm supposed to drink from it without so much as a drop of soap? Bottoms up!

The wedding surprised me again when later a gentleman dipped a spoon into a huge bowl of some brown goop and offered it to me. I had to stop and ask him how to eat it, so he gestured that I take the spoon and put it in my mouth. Why didn't I think of that! After doing so, he dipped the spoon back into the bowl of goop and offered it to the next guy in line. Sure, it was delicious, but I can't think about the process too much without a bit of nausea!

In the end, I guess I'd rather volunteer to do the dishes. I hate washing dishes, but somehow a little bit of soap repels repulsive reactions. Life is different here, and that's just another Monday in the Middle East.

October 31, 2005 – Sit-n-Stare/Eat-n-Go

I mentioned last week how I got to experience my first Arab wedding a while back. I call it the Sit-n-Stare/Eat-n-

Go wedding. It was definitely not a typical church wedding with the bride and groom taking vows in front of a grand cathedral. First of all, there certainly was no church, and there wasn't even a mosque. In fact, there wasn't much of anything religious. I guess you could say it was more of a social occasion rather than a religious one, but, nonetheless, it left an impression on me.

I walked into a large rented hall where the groom and his father, brothers, grandfather, and uncles were all dressed in costly regalia, greeting people at the door. As we filed in, we were all seated in rows of seats facing one another. This gave me a feeling kind of like waiting for a transfer in a Greyhound bus station. What a wonderful opportunity to sit and stare at old men I'd never met! Notwithstanding, I met a nice fellow and enjoyed a good bit of conversation.

Suddenly, there was a fire alarm and everyone evacuated the room like they were being chased by a herd of raging sheep! Come to find out, it was not a fire alarm, but rather, a simple announcement that the food was ready in another room. Everybody up! Everybody move! Everybody sit! Everybody eat! These men wasted no time devouring the delicious food in front of them. Normally, the same men would eat any other meal seated on plastic mats on the floor using their hands as the only utensils on hand, but at this occasion, we sat at tables and had the full spread of multiple forks, spoons, knives, and cups. They made light work of the meal, then . . . they left! A few of them stopped to greet the groom before departing, but most of them just wiped their mouths and spoofed.

From my western perspective, there was something strange about this. Sure, there's the sanitation issue I mentioned last week, then there was the quick meal with desserts, but something was noticeably absent: women! You'd think that at least there would be a bride and maybe even a ceremony to legally unite the bride and groom, but alas, there was not. Despite my wife's assurance that there were, indeed, women and a bride in another room, I can't say I saw a whole Arab wedding. Whatever happened to "before these witnesses, I now pronounce you husband and wife"? That makes me wonder, have Arabs even witnessed a whole Arab wedding? I guess this bride and groom will have to count their own wedding as the only wedding they've really witnessed. Well, life is different here, and that's just another Monday in the Middle East.

November 7, 2005 –
Birth by Email! Mideast Meets Midwest

My wife and I are thrilled at the arrival of our fourth child, a little boy just a bit over a week ago. Our other three kids were born in the same U.S. hospital with the same doctor and even the same attending nurse. In other words, we knew we were in for a new experience besides being 8,000 miles (as the crow flies) from everything familiar.

One of the first surprises was when the nurse explained a few months ago the different things my wife needed to bring along to the hospital. She added to the list, "Bring your husband, too, or at least some man who can sign the papers." Maybe it was a foregone conclusion that I would be present. Even so, it's good to know that I could have been replaced by any male friend or even a taxi driver just in case. But what if there was no male to sign the papers? "Wait, wait! Don't give birth yet! Your husband hasn't arrived!"

I was, in fact, present throughout the delivery, but I still wanted to keep the family back in the Midwest updated on our birth in the Mideast. Then I realized I had my trusty Pocket PC PDA with wireless capability! What a blessing for this desert delivery! I periodically stepped out of the delivery room to the church parking lot next door to "borrow" some wireless Internet access.

"Contractions are getting stronger . . . ."

"We've been admitted to the hospital . . . ."

"Looks like a C-section is necessary . . . ."
"It's a boy!"
Birth by email!

I was there through the days to follow, too. To be sure, I was there every 3-4 hours with little choice in the matter. You see, the hospital stay doesn't include meals even for patients. Instead, the nurses and doctors told me what I could bring so that my wife could eat, and I made special order trips to the grocery store. Back and forth I went getting the soup, and the specific fruit, and the special drinks. Where's "Simon Delivers" when you need it? Grocery delivery would have been great at least to get some food on the table. I had the Internet access; I could have placed a full order!

There I go again applying my Western mindset on our Middle Eastern experience. From another perspective, look at the incredible family unit. It is basically a prerequisite that your family be present if you go to the hospital. Individuals are so culturally connected to their families that it's unthinkable that someone would be at the hospital without family to provide meals. In fact, it was only 30-40 years ago that the outside of this hospital grounds doubled as a campground! That's right, the Bedouin families from the desert who made journeys of days and days by camel just to get to the hospital needed a place to stay, so they set up camp right on the hospital grounds. Of course, they brought food for the whole clan, so why wouldn't they take it into the hospital for the patient? That's what families do, isn't it? They provide for each other and stick by each other.

Maybe the next time I'm in the hospital I'll order out. I won't be calling Pizza Hut for delivery, though. Nah, I'll call my sister back home and say, "Get on a plane and bring me some food! I'm hungry!"

Life is different here, and that's just another Monday in the Middle East.

November 14, 2005 – Lather Up in the Great Outdoors

The Islamic prophet Mohammed once said his two weaknesses were scents and women. I guess I have to say the "scents" thing surprises me.

In one sense, the Arab world has some of the best, most intense perfumes I've ever encountered. Some women pass by and leave a fragrant wake that follows 10-12 feet after. A person could squander a small fortune on beautiful blown-glass flasks filled with scents that could understandably make someone weak.

On the other hand, the Middle East is home to a lot of hot, sweaty people, Americans included. For seven months of the year the daily high temperatures exceed 100 degrees which makes this land an outright B.O. factory! Yeah, the scents could certainly make people weak—as in dizzy and about to fall over.

Yesterday, though, I met an industrious farmer who did his part to combat this trend. We visited a palm tree oasis where irrigation channels are used to harness the natural spring water for the farm. These two-foot-wide channels allow thousands of trees to be watered without the need for pumps or anything other than gravity.

As I was walking along the channel I asked the farmer a few questions about the irrigation which he kindly answered as he went about his business. Suddenly, I heard him exclaim, "Oooof!" and I turned around to find him sitting down fully clothed in the irrigation channel! I asked him if he fell as he splashed around, but he said, "No! I've been working hard all day and I needed to get cleaned up!" Sure enough, he even had a bar of Lux soap sitting beside him.

Now that's creative, isn't it? Why waste time doing laundry AND bathing when you can kill two birds with one stone irrigation channel?

Life is different here, and that's just another Monday in the Middle East.

November 21, 2005 – Sports and Chemical Weapons

I noticed this past week that back in the Midwest you got your first real taste of winter. We got our first real taste of winter, too. From the first week of April to the last week of October, we can count on an unbroken chain of 100+ degree days, and the chain is finally broken.

I really feel sorry for all of you suffering with highs in the 20's though. Can you feel the oozing empathy? Here's a story to keep you warm with laughter.

This past summer my family and I spent a month working in the tiny island nation of Bahrain here in the Arabian Gulf. We had lived in Bahrain for a year, and I'd heard of a friend who walked across the country—before church. Have you ever considered walking across the country before the 10 a.m. service?

I decided that on this trip to Bahrain I was going to make my cross-country pilgrimage whether the circumstances were favorable or not. Well, the circumstances were . . . "NOT."

There are two months of the year when even locals leave the Middle East, namely, July and August with August being the worst because even the sea temperatures climb to a whopping 96-97 degrees. Suddenly, jumping into the water to cool off takes on a whole new meaning akin to Jacuzzi. Considering this, an island nation like Bahrain sees constant humidity of about 97-99% and this day was no different.

I stepped out of the house at 2 p.m. into stifling 107 degree weather. Three and a half hours and eleven miles later, I dipped my Vasque hiking boots into the algae covered shores on the other side of the island. I measured the liquids I consumed in gallons which made me feel more like a car than a hiker! When I told the taxi driver on the return trip home that I'd just walked across the country, he said, "Across the country? That's far! Are you crazy?"

Yeah, a little bit, and more of the story proves it. Needless to say, my legs were burning and aching, so I took my family to a drug store to buy some sports cream. They didn't have anything familiar, so I took what they had.

Mistake #1: When in need of urgent medical care, don't trust a pharmacist (Indian) speaking a second language (Arabic) recommending a product (French) with no explanation in your first language (English).

I quickly excused myself to the restroom to apply this sports cream generously to my aching calves and thighs, then rejoined my family to drive out to eat a celebratory meal.

About ten minutes later just as the cream started to kick in and I realized we were stuck in traffic, I made a painful discovery.

Mistake #2: Read the label for warnings against use in extreme climates.

It's 107 degrees outside, with 98% humidity. Human cell metabolism is only 60% efficient and I've just walked 11 miles in blistering heat. Discovery: Any chemical reaction that the sports cream might normally cause will be magnitudes faster and stronger than normal conditions!

Mistake #3: Even if product has no caution against use in extreme climates, use your head!

"Aaaaggghhhhhh! My legs are burning! I've got to get these slacks off! Aaaghhh! I'm in rush hour traffic! I'm getting chemical burns on my legs! Get me outta here!"

We made an emergency stop at a mall where I bought the first pair of shorts I set eyes on. "Price doesn't matter! Just give me the shorts!" Off I went dashing to the restroom to scrub the fire from my skin with paper towels or toilet paper or whatever. Too late. The damage was done. I walked out of there with my new shorts revealing my beet-red legs with a chemical burn that rivaled my worst sunburn ever.

It was quite a lesson in chemistry that day that I won't soon forget. Just keep in mind that all of those annoying high school calculations in moles and energy do have a purpose, particularly in moles of sports cream!

Life is different here, and that's just another Monday in the Middle East.

November 28, 2005 – My Very Own Harem?

One of the traditions of nomadic Arabs is to slaughter most of the male camels shortly after birth. These Bedouin people live on camel's milk in the harsh deserts of Arabia, so why would they waste precious food and water on camels that will never bring forth milk or more camels? Consequently, male camels are in high demand for their, uh, services. I guess you could call it justified camel polygamy.

It seems that some of that camel wisdom has spread into Arab marriage as well. No, no, not the offspring thing, but the polygamy! As hard as it is for us Westerners to get our minds around it, polygamy is a fact of life here. Most Muslim men are restricted to four wives, although the religion's founder took 13. The most I've heard of, though, is forty-six wives to one man, my Saudi friend's grandfather. My friend was careful to explain, "Oh, not all at the same time! Only four wives at one time, but he just divorced that many." However you look at it, his 70+ children makes for a lot of diapers.

I'm convinced the Arabs I know want to hook me up with some more wives, too. We were visiting friends at the hospital when the woman's sister remarked that with four children, we are like an Omani family. The she said to my wife, Cheryl, "God willing, you will have ten children."

My wife responded, "Ten children??? I'm tired after four!"

The woman then pointed to me and said, "No, no, *he* can have ten. You just have to have four."

Yikes.

This past week I was at a hospital where I was talking with a 50-year-old woman and a 25-year-old woman. The older woman complimented my Arabic, saying one year of study was enough for me and I didn't need another year. Then she added while gesturing at the younger woman, "If you study another year, we'll give you an Arab passport! And you can marry a local girl like this!"

Yikes! I explained that I am already married with four children, but it didn't stop her "match made in Arabia." She even moved to a different seat and told the younger woman to sit on the couch next to me.

I don't think that would quite work out like she'd planned, though, and my Arabic lessons prove it. As my Arabic language helper and I were discussing Arab polygamy one day, he jested that maybe I should marry three or four wives. Then he sat back, tapped his chin with his finger, and said matter-of-factly, "No, I think if you would marry a second wife, Cheryl would kill you!"

Yep, I think he's right about that. So much for this harem that people are planning for me.

Life is different here, and that's just another Monday in the Middle East.

December 5, 2005 – Just Another Manic . . . Saturday?

I've never been to Israel, but I have learned a few things about Jerusalem, a.k.a. "the city that never sleeps." The fact that Jerusalem is the center of the world's three great monotheistic religions means that the title is rightfully it's own. You see, the Muslims keep Friday as their holy day, the Jews keep Saturday as their holy day, and the Christians keep Sunday as their holy day. On any one of those three days, two-thirds of the city is still bustling about like any other day while one-third is resting. The city never sleeps!

I suppose one of the ironic things about <u>Mondays in the Middle East</u> is that it is named for an emotion that never really happens here. In the U.S., the nearest thing to a national holy day is Sunday which makes Monday the dreaded day to return to work. So when I say it's "just another Monday in the Middle East," it's supposed to conjure up the emotion of another goofy start to the week when anything can go wrong and usually does. In reality, Monday isn't the day of drudgery here that it is in the U.S., so the emotion is never actually there.

Nope, since Friday is the Muslims' holy day, the weekend here is Thursday and Friday when most people stop working. However, in Cairo, the weekend is Friday and Saturday. It gets really confusing when you take your feelings for Monday and apply them to Saturday, unless you're in Cairo, in which case your Monday feelings would fall on Sunday. So Monday is actually more like a Wednesday and Saturday takes the place of Monday. Even Friday is messed up because, here, that's Wednesday. You're happy about the weekend at hand on Friday? We're already dreading work on Saturday!

What's funny about it is the Arabic names for the days of the week. Sunday is actually called "the first day" even though it's not the first day of the week. What's really strange is that the Arabic word for Saturday is Sabbath, just like the Jews.

I bet Middle Eastern stock brokers could easily develop a complex with this bizarre calendar business; their jobs are Monday to Friday even though the rest of the Middle East has a weekend anytime from Friday through Sunday. I wonder how many people get counseling over this before returning to the West.

When I take my kids to church for Friday worship services, do they go to "Friday School" or do they go to "Sunday School" that meets on Friday? I'd better play it safe and just call it "Church School."

Whereas I'm as mixed up as ever, this could really work to the advantage of one place in the world; someone's always awake for your business in the city that never sleeps.

Life is different here, and that's just another Monday in the Middle East. Or is it?

December 12, 2005 – A Glimpse of Heaven

Last week I mentioned the church services on Friday, and it is a bit of an adjustment to have "the Lord's Day" on anything but Sunday. Yet, this is the way it is for most churches in the Middle East. Friday is the Muslim holy day, so Muslim governments give Friday off of work.

It's not the only day for church for some folks, though. In fact, one church I'm familiar with in Bahrain has almost thirty different congregations meeting in the same building complex throughout the week. Now that's getting the most out of your church building! These congregations span across seven official languages that the church supports (although there are more unofficial language congregations), and numerous denominations. You've got everything from a Pentecostal Filipino congregation to a conservative Indian fellowship to a traditional Reformed American congregation.

I really have to qualify that "American congregation" bit, though. Yes, the church was started by Americans over 100 years ago, and yes, there is an American pastor there now. However, the church is mostly Indian even though it is the main English-speaking congregation in the country.

The church I attend in the United Arab Emirates is very similar, but I think 1 could say it is even more heterogeneous. Recently the pastor had everyone stand up in the service. Then he had people sit down as he listed off the countries he thought might be represented. In the end, there were twenty-eight different countries represented in the English language congregation alone! That's one international mix if you ask me.

It's a real witness, though. Twenty-eight countries represent dozens of home languages, and they all come together for English worship. It's quite a place with some great worship. Where else could you find a middle-aged Indian woman dressed in her sari jamming away on an electric guitar leading worship for 350 people from all over the world? I'd say you'd be hard pressed to find that sort of thing this side of heaven.

If you're on the building committee of your church, though, maybe this could be of some encouragement to you. You could propose that a couple dozen churches could use one church complex to its maximum potential. How would that idea fly? Congregations meeting one after the other the whole day through? The whole week through?

Life is different here, and that's just another Monday in the Middle East.

December 19, 2005 – Lights Without Clothes On

My two-year-old daughter is doing very well learning English these days, even when people all around her are speaking dozens of different languages. She knows what "no" means, she knows what "lights" are, and she even knows what "naked" means. On the other hand, she would have been as bewildered as I was when I read a sign that said, "No Naked Lights!" What in the world does that mean? This completely unfamiliar phrase only made sense to me when I noticed that it was posted on a fuel truck. Ahh, now I get it. You meant, "No Open Flames," but you weren't telling me to dress my fluorescent light bulb in high heels and a skirt!

Some folks here can use a lesson in this new lingo, too. The houses here don't have natural gas lines that snake to each house underground. No, no, the system is much more basic than that. You pay a deposit for a large cylinder that sits outside your kitchen window, and the gas hose strings directly to your oven from there. I imagine this system saves a lot of money when compared to establishing a vast natural gas piping infrastructure.

Still, we were amazed that our cylinder lasted a whopping ten months without needing to be refilled. Elijah had his olive oil, well, we have our natural gas! This blessing did come to an end, though, so I chased down the gas truck that drives around with refill cylinders. Normally, we hear the annoying horn of this gas truck sounding through the neighborhood at least once a day, but when we really needed to do some cooking, his beep-beep-beep-beep-beep-beep-beep was noticeably absent for three days. Not to be deterred, I jumped in my car, drove around until I found the gas man, and led him back to our house.

Rather than accepting my help in carrying the tank, he just dropped it off the back of the truck, threw it down on its side, and proceeded to make an awful ruckus by rolling it on the concrete all the way around to the back of the house. All the while, I kept thinking, "Wow, those tanks must be pretty strong, but, hey, he knows what he's doing."

After unhooking the gas line from the old tank, he cranked the hose nozzle onto the new one. I'm sure I could have done it myself, but I gladly let him do it since he was the expert. He carefully tightened the nozzle onto the tank, then stopped talking and put his ear to the nozzle. Again, I thought, "Well, I'm glad he's doing this because I might not have thought to listen for any leaks. He's sure got the experience."

His next step cast serious doubt on all the credibility I'd just given him. I'd already started to walk around the house because I thought he was done, but his next move just about made me dive for cover. Think about it; here's a metal tank compressed with an explosive gas, so why would he ever take out a lighter and wave a flame around the nozzle??? "Hey! No naked lights!" I'm no genius, but there has got to be a better way to check for leaks on a gas tank!

What can I say, life is different here, and that's just another Monday in the Middle East.

December 26, 2005 – Welcome in the Middle East!

Despite what U.S. news broadcasters would have you believe, the Middle East is actually a very friendly place. Even though the grammar of the phrase isn't quite on track, I've heard over and over, "Welcome in the Middle East!" or "Welcome in Egypt!" or "Welcome in Bahrain!" Other than making me question who taught these people English, this friendly expression has led me to believe people really want to get to know Americans.

One of my friends here had a similar experience in a taxi. As they got going on their roller coaster ride through the city, the taxi driver asked my friend where he was from.

"America," he answered.

The taxi driver responded, "Oh, you Americans are different from us Arabs." Hmm, really? How's that (other than the language, the culture, the religion, the race, and the ethnicity)?

"Arabs are more friendly than Americans. Arabs are friends with everyone, even people we don't know." Oh really? How's that?

"Watch," said the taxi driver as he rolled down his window. Then with the agility of a monkey in a zoo he drove the car with one hand while leaning half his body out the window to wave wildly at a poor bystander. "*Salaam alaykum!*" he yelled. This greeting ("Peace be on you") is as common as "Hello" and the response is normally a warm, friendly "*Alaykum asalam,*" in return. This time, though, the bewildered response, "*Alaykum asalam?*" seemed to convey the meaning, "You're crazy! Is this what you want me to say?" No sooner had the driver gotten the desired response than he plopped back in his seat and said, "See, now we're friends!"

Welcome in Oman. Life is different here, and that's just another Monday in the Middle East.

January 2, 2006 – Walk Across a City

I mentioned last week how "friendly" the Middle East is, but it's even more friendly than getting someone to respond after yelling "Hello!" out the window.

For example, take Adel, a shop owner in one of the southern suburbs of Cairo. Years ago I used my day off for a long subway ride to a museum of ancient Bible manuscripts only to find that the museum was closed that day; so I was turned away at the door. Dandy. Head hanging and shoulders drooping, I walked down the street until Adel invited me into his shop of all sorts of tourist wares. After talking a while I noticed his nice prayer rug folded up by his desk. Muslims use these prayer rugs to spread out on the ground to kneel and pray for their five prayers each day. I'd seen a bunch of cheap carpets being sold in these tourist shops, but this one was really nice, so I asked him in my limited Arabic, "How much?" He said, "No, no, this is not for sale." I tried to explain in Arabic that I wasn't trying to buy this one but I just wanted an idea of how much those types of carpets cost. Still, since I didn't know all of the words, I ended up asking again, "How much?" Adel was very courteous to this foreigner trying to buy his prayer rug right out from under him, and he again explained, "This one isn't for sale. I'll take you to a carpet shop."

So off we walked . . . for about an hour! Finally we got to the carpet factory with the same cheap carpets I mentioned earlier, but none of the nice ones. I ended up buying one of those carpets just to make it worth Adel's time, and we continued to walk on toward Cairo. This was my personal tour of the places tourists never see, like Garbage City. Here, the residents live in shanties and collect trash from the streets of Cairo to fuel pottery kilns. Looking through the black, carcinogenic smoke of the burning plastic I saw a very friendly toothless man who was glad to explain to me how his feet had been spinning this wheel since he was a child, churning out one hundred pots and vases a day. Never mind that he's only in his mid-thirties and he's likely to live only five or ten more years.

Adel and I continued to walk on . . . for five or six hours that day. I repeatedly offered to pay for a bus ride or a subway ride or a taxi ride, but he repeatedly refused. In hindsight I can see that I was his guest, and it would have been dishonorable to allow me to pay for anything, no matter how trivial. So on we walked.

In fact, even though my flight to Egypt cost three times his annual wage, Adel bought me lunch. It certainly wasn't at a five-star hotel, but his generosity even in this small thing was magnanimous.

In the end, we went our separate ways near his home. So what did this shop owner ask in return for this five hour walk across a city? "When you go back to America, just remember me."

Adel, I remember. Thank you. Life is different here, and that's just another Monday in the Middle East.

January 9, 2006 –
Backseat Drivers, Got Plans for the Next Six Months?
We're all familiar with the concept of backseat drivers, but it takes a new meaning here. Your wife may still stomp on the imaginary brake at the floorboards, and your kids will still yell, "It's green!" the instant the light turns, but now you've got other drivers beeping and barking at you to do the same. If you pull up to a line of cars at a traffic light and you don't move forward that extra 3-5 feet to the next vehicle, the gentleman behind you will blast his horn to let you know, "You've got three feet you could move forward!" It's like having backseat drivers in other cars!

Another peculiarity here is the habit of flashing your bright lights when approaching a slower vehicle to let them know you want to get by. If that vehicle is in the left lane, it should move to the right. If that vehicle is in the right lane, it should move to the right. I still don't understand how this is safe when two cars in oncoming traffic may each be forced onto the shoulder by two speeders in oncoming traffic who want to play Chicken on a two-lane road.

One fellow who did this recently didn't know that the vehicle he wanted to pass was driven by an off-duty police officer. The cop was moving at the speed limit, so he didn't move to the right. The speeding driver became irate and moved into the right lane to make a certain hand gesture that got him six-months' free meals in the local jail.

Isn't it interesting that an on-duty police officer won't pull you over for speeding, but even an off-duty officer can escort you to the clink without passing "Go" and without collecting $200? Somebody's got all the cards in this monopoly, and it's not the hot-tempered backseat drivers in other cars.

Tickets really are a strange thing here. You can even get a ticket for not having a clean car, so I bet this guy is thankful for one last car wash beforehand. That would be adding insult to injury: "Six months jail. Oh yeah, a $30 fine for a dirty car." Life is different here, and that's just another Monday in the Middle East.

January 16, 2006 –
"Don't Hate Me Because I'm Beautiful."

We've all seen how little babies tucked in their cute little bundles of blankets with their chubby little cheeks draw people in. Since my family's white skin and blond hair is a slim minority here, our children certainly draw attention, but especially our newborn. Fully-veiled women might hide their faces, but they can't hide the squint of their smiling eyes! With all of their smiles and questions about our children, they always say, *"Maashallah,"* which means, "What God wills!" In this particular circumstance, they are complimenting our children, but the compliment must be given indirectly. The common belief is that if they would say, "What a beautiful baby," they might put a curse on the child by drawing the attention of jinn (think of a genie in a bottle, only without the three wishes)!

This is one reason it is important *not* to compliment people. For instance, I don't wear a wrist watch in the Middle East because of the intense summer heat. The heat tends to give heat rash and . . . well . . . a stinky wrist right around the band. Nevertheless, I once complimented a friend's watch. A few days later I saw him with a new watch, and he gave me his old watch! Since I'd complimented his watch, he felt obligated to give it to me. Plus, I'd just brought the attention of jinn to it. Better to give the thing away than wear a watch that might have the evil eye watching it. The same principle applies to people, too. Well, the jinn part at least. If you compliment someone on looks, don't expect the person to be given to you! Still, the person may not appreciate that you've brought the attention of jinn.

"*Maashallah*" is the security blanket to protect against these ills. Simply acknowledge that God has given it, and you don't have to worry about those nasty jinn. "*Maashallah*" acknowledges that God gives many things.

If you get the flu from shaking hands with someone, "*Maashallah*," God willed it. The fact that you didn't wash your hands has little to do with it. God willed it.

If you find a $100 bill on the ground, "*Maashallah*," God willed it. No need to try to find the owner. God wanted you to have it.

If you drive a $500 Ford Escort and your neighbor drives an $80,000 Hummer, "*Maashallah*," God wants you to drive an Escort.

On the other hand, if God wills me to have a Hummer, "*Maashallah*! Free dune rides for everyone!"

I could even say, "*Maashallah*," life is different here, and that's just another Monday in the Middle East.

January 23, 2006 – Middle Eastern Lingerie
Standards of modesty vary so widely from culture to culture that it's hard to keep track of them. Two of our friends were the first people with white skin ever to set foot in a certain village in the Far East. The trouble was that no one there wore a single stitch of clothes. This bit of "culture shock" was such a challenge that the wife of this couple bought a pair of shorts and a belt to present as a gift to the village chief. The chief

was very grateful, and the next day he showed up proudly sporting his new outfit: a belt! He threw away the shorts, but the belt, he treasured for years to come.

I suppose the Middle East defines the other end of this modesty spectrum. There are some cities here that are scarcely different than Chicago, Milwaukee, or Minneapolis, but in our city both men and women dress very modestly. Dresses extending from wrist-to-wrist and neck-to-floor are the norm. In fact, I saw one store filled wall to wall with nothing but these dresses. Granted, they were beautiful dresses, but I had to laugh when I stepped back to see written on the window, "Lingerie"! That word now has a totally new meaning.

What's confusing is the difference between lingerie, house dresses, and formal dresses. They are all wrist-to-wrist, neck-to-floor dresses, so what's the dividing line? My wife discovered this fine line when she wore an Arab dress to the mall. It was obviously a conservative dress, but why did people stare at her? People looked at her as if to say, "Why is she wearing that??" After asking an Arab friend later, she found that what she wore was a house dress, which wouldn't be worn outside without wearing a full black *abayya* over it. Whew! At least she hadn't mistakenly worn lingerie!

For all the women considering a visit to the Middle East, here's a word to the wise: know thy clothes. They might seem identical to you, but here dresses are different which makes this just another Monday in the Middle East.

January 30, 2006 – Off the Shelf Politics

For years I sat down each morning to eat bread and peanut butter dipped in cocoa for breakfast. Strange, maybe, but I even confessed this habit to my wife before I married her. Recently, the doctor encouraged me to give up my main breakfast staple for cholesterol-lowering foods like oatmeal. Yum. So I walked to the store tonight to load up on oatmeal, but, strangely, I couldn't find the oats where I'd seen them before. I was sure I'd seen them here on that shelf before and I'd even seen them on end-caps for special bulk sale. "Hmm," I thought, "I'd better ask."

"Do you have oatmeal?"

"Yes, I have," replied the store manager, and he walked me to a back corner of the store. "We've been told to take everything from Denmark off the shelves. Something about them refusing to sell the Koran or something."

Suddenly I felt like I was in a "gun" shop in Britain where I was shown the goods on the bottom shelf in the back corner of the store. I felt like maybe I should do a double-take over my shoulder and lower my voice to ask, "Do you have anything with a bit more punch to it like *honey*-flavored oatmeal?" You know, it's important to get just the right caliber of goods when you're buying things under the table.

Maybe this whole politics/religion thing is a bit strange, but it shows how political issues thousands of miles away can have a huge influence in a community culture like the Middle East. One of my friends lived in Jordan for some time during the 90's. For some reason, only Pepsi products were on the shelves and only Pepsi products were advertised on the streets. My friend left the country for about a week, and when he returned, Coca-Cola was on every billboard and in every little store wherever he went! What was the difference? Apparently, Coke had been selling to Israel whereas Pepsi had not. Friends of Israel are no friends of the Middle East, so no Coke. During that particular week, Coke saw the light and gave up Israel for the much bigger Middle Eastern market. Suddenly, Arabs were permitted to enjoy fully the "delicious, refreshing" drink.

Take heed Wisconsin. You might be sitting on a whole lot of aged cheese if you mock those Golden Gophers. On second thought, Minneapolis will always have some shady, back-alley shop to sell cheddar. Go to the back corner and check the bottom shelf.

Hey, life is different here, and that's just another Monday in the Middle East.

February 6, 2006 – Kleenex, Kleenex Everywhere!

One thing known about Americans the world over is that we love our paper. It's no pulp fiction to say that this fixation for paper stretches from the toilet to the table, from the tissue box to the tool box. We've got a type of paper for everything and a roll, box, dispenser, or all of the above wherever we need it.

Our family has taken on a new interpretation of the paper frenzy. Yes, we are Americans, so we have to have our paper. Yet, we've found a new approach, namely, the common Middle Eastern habit of using ordinary tissues for everything out of the ordinary. Sure, we'll use napkins when we can get them, but we went for months without seeing them in stores. What did we do? "When in Rome . . . " do as the Arabs do. Use tissues.

I'll even teach you an Arabic word to demonstrate how pervasive these boxes are: *kaleeneks*. Need the translation? It means:

- table napkin
- paper towel
- toilet paper (better 'n nothing)
- wipe for cleaning house windows
- hand towel in public restrooms
- eyeglass cleaner ("the whole world streaked before my eyes")
- windshield cleaner
- towel to clean medical instruments (BEFORE a more thorough sterilization process)
- shop towel for checking oil

If that Arabic word is too hard to remember, try this one: *teeshoo*. Either way, this is one of the most versatile items money can buy in this part of the world. And if you share the common expectation of "a paper for everything, and every paper in its place," well, this may be the only paper you can get.

I sat down in a friend's beautiful new BMW decked with soft leather interior throughout, ceiling and all. Then I noticed the clunky wire contraption hanging from the ceiling above the center rear-view mirror. I chuckled a bit to see this luxurious, top-of-the-line car with a little wire holder clamped down on a box of, you guessed it, Kleenex. Hey, what does aesthetics matter if you don't have a tissue to wipe your eyes with? Who knows; of the myriad uses for Kleenex, you might even decide to blow your nose.

Life is different here, and that's just another Monday in the Middle East.

February 13, 2006 – Passport Control

My first overseas travels took me to Romania in 1992. We took this trip only a year and a half after the fall of communism, and we were warned that there was already a black market for stolen U.S. passports. "Guard your passport at all times. Never give it to anyone, and if you really have to hand it over, don't let it out of your sight."

So, like any green, American traveler I didn't trust anyone with my passport. I even followed immigration officials around when they took my passport. After all, I wasn't going to let it out of my sight!

The Middle East is a totally different ball game. For instance, when traveling through Saudi Arabia, you surrender your passport at the point of entry, drive to your point of exit, and pray that your passport arrives before you're ready to leave. Even in other Gulf countries employers regularly take employees' passports when they arrive in country, and they don't return them until employment is terminated. You might go months or years without seeing your passport.

One of my friends taught for over 10 years in a Middle Eastern university. In the last weeks when he'd resigned from his job, he didn't see his passport, nor his wife's, nor his children's. Nope, all of the passports were in the hands of his employer until their departure time when his employer drove the family to the airport and handed the passports to the immigration official. What was my friend's perspective on this? "There's not a lot of trust around here." Well, not much more than I gave Romanian immigration.

I've softened quite a bit, though. Recently, some relatives visited from the U.S., so we rented some four-wheelers for a special trip to the dunes. As collateral against damage I had to leave my passport with the rental shop, but I knew my family and I weren't going to destroy these four-wheelers. No problem.

After five hours of dune bashing we decided we'd better wrap things up. "Just one more trip around!" So, my brother-in-law tried to climb the biggest dune in sight at full throttle on that last trek through the sand. Wouldn't you know it, he suddenly jerked to a stop and was nearly thrown over the handle bars! No joke, the four-wheeler had broken in half! We were sweating something fierce as we dragged the crippled ATV down the dune, and it wasn't just because of exertion. How do you explain something like this to the rental shop? "Well, you see, it just broke . . . in half!"

We hemmed and hawed with the owner until finally we negotiated a reasonable price for the cost of a new A-frame. I tell you, I didn't care how much it cost; it was a serious sigh of relief when I slapped down the money, and the owner slapped down my passport. Middle Eastern passport control.

Hey, life is different here, and that's just another Monday in the Middle East.

February 20, 2006 – Coming Clean

Just a few days ago I met a friend whom I hadn't seen for a while, but I noticed his short hair cut. I gave him the customary greeting given to someone who has just had a haircut, namely, "You've cleaned!" Americans might otherwise say, "Ahh, sharp looking haircut!" Yet, here the response isn't a mere "Thank you" but rather "May God clean you!"

The interchange is the same after someone has just gotten out of the shower, "Ahh, you've cleaned!" For me, I laugh each time I think of this because you never can tell what is meant by the response phrase, "May God clean you!" What goes through my mind is some sort of one-upmanship. The first guy says, "You've finally taken a shower!" Then the second retorts, "May God clean you; you really need it."

The whole scenario gets really interesting when you consider Islamic laws for cleanliness. Each time they pray, Muslims wash their hands to their elbows, their feet to their ankles, and their faces back to their ears. That's all fine and well until you come to the part of the regulation that says if water is not available for these ablutions, you may use sand or even fine dirt for this "washing." That's right, no Purell hand sanitizer, no soap, no water—just sand or dirt to scrub up.

As for me, when I was a kid, my mother made me wash up BECAUSE of the fine dirt behind my ears! In fact, if I had dirt on my hands up to my elbows, on my feet up to my ankles, and on my face back to my ears, Splish! Splash! I'd be takin' a bath, even if it wasn't a Saturday night!

Yeah, I would struggle with this sand/dirt cleaning approach. If my son comes in from playing outside and I say, "Son, you're filthy! Go outside and roll in the dirt to get yourself clean;" he might say, "But, Daddy, I just did!"

Then what would I say? "Ahh, you've cleaned!" Life is different here, and that's just another Monday in the Middle East.

February 27, 2006 – Wake Up, O Sleeper!

When traveling overseas, certain elements of the new culture you are experiencing will seem like everyday life and others will just plain shock you. In the Middle East, the call to prayer is one of those things that just might knock you back to the Middle Ages! Muslims are required to pray five times each day just as they have for 1400 years, and the call to prayer is an audible reminder to pray. It's not a telephone call, but it grabs your attention no less as a *muezzin* chants the call from the mosque towers. The first call to prayer of the day is given at the moment when a white thread can be distinguished from a black thread at arm's length. The time of this reminder can vary depending on things like the time of year or whether the *muezzin* can find his glasses. Back when Islam started in A.D. 622, the *muezzin* must have had very reliable roosters, but today, computer models predict the very minute of the call to prayer in cities around the world years in advance. Tape recorders replace the human element by automatically beginning the chant without the need for anyone to be present. In a place like Cairo, the call to prayer can be heard moving across the city in a wall of sound as each mosque begins only a moment after the previous one.

I'd experienced this wall of sound in Egypt, so I should have known what was coming on our first visit to Bahrain. We visited in March when the desert weather was picturesque with 70-degree-nights to lull us to sleep. On account of this, my wife and I enjoyed the cool breeze by sleeping with the windows wide open. We discovered the next morning that this is a mistake for visitors. At 4:15 a.m. we both shot straight up in bed because of an eerie shouting coming through the window! No, it wasn't a thief in the night, but, rather, the mosque across the street. Without fail, it wakes Muslims every day at sunrise with the voice of the recorded *muezzin* blaring through loud speakers. Unfortunately for us, it wakes the non-Muslims, too. Welcome to Bahrain! Life is certainly different here, and that's just another Monday in the Middle East.

March 6, 2006 – Bathroom Gratuity

One of the challenges with potty training a two-year-old is specifying how much of what goes where. It's obvious where some things go; that's the point of potty training, right? On the other hand, a two-year-old may not calculate what happens when she fills the toilet with a whole package of baby wipes, then flushes them *en masse*. An experienced plumber knows, though, and it took our plumber about 10-15 minutes trying to clear the foul, knee-deep flood outside our bathroom window. I watched him struggle to shove a long plastic tube through the pipes to clear the blockage, and suddenly I heard a huge gush of . . . stuff . . . and the first thing the plumber cried out was, "Tip!" Normally, in the Middle East people ask for tips for the smallest bit of assistance they might give, but this time I didn't reach for coins; I pulled out my wallet. Hey, you've earned it, pal.

If anyone is in need of gratuity training, a few weeks in Egypt will serve as your perfect instructor. Gratuities are expected for meals and camel rides but they're also expected for as small a thing as allowing me to take a picture of a camel, or handing me a towelette in a restroom. That being said, I was nonetheless shocked by a "gratuity" experience in the beautiful city of Alexandria, Egypt. After a nice meal of spaghetti at a seashore restaurant with five or six friends, I found myself in need of a restroom. I was innocently walking to the bathroom when a waitress noticed me, left the two other waitresses she was with, and immediately got in step behind me. Methinks, "OK, maybe she's planning to stop at the doorway and wait until I wash my hands to give me a towel to dry my hands with." She showed she had different plans by walking straight into the restroom after me. Alas, in front of me, though, was a table with a bunch of towelettes laid out. Methinks further, "OK, well, she is really into her job and wants to be right there when I'm through washing my hands, so I'll just take a few more steps in and she'll wait there." Following suit, *she* took a few steps in so that she stood in full view of me and the urinals! I spun around hoping to drive her away with my bewildered look, but, instead, I met a face blanketed with a peculiar, interested smile. In total astonishment, I turned and entered the stall instead of using the urinals and gave it a noticeable slam in yet another attempt to scare her off. "What audacity," I thought. "How could she do such a thing? They don't even do this in the States!" As I left the stall I thought again that surely she would have realized her error and walked out in embarrasm—There she was again with that questioning smile!! I still have no idea what she was doing, but, hey, I've got another story to illustrate just how different life is here where that's just another Monday in the Middle East!

March 13, 2006 – "That's Pretty Slick!"

Having worked in technology for seven years, I get pretty excited about new gadgets, but I have to admit that I like nice, simple examples of efficiency, too.

Shortly after we arrived here we had some furniture delivered to our house. As is the common custom, the delivery men also assembled the furniture, so I got to see their toolboxes. On the other hand, can you call a plastic grocery bag inside of another plastic grocery bag a "toolbox"? Whatever does the job, I suppose. Soon I started to notice all sorts of car mechanics, plumbers, and carpenters with their "toolboxes," so I did the same and saved myself spending 20 bucks on a fancy plastic box. Now if my toolbox wears out, I grab two more plastic bags and I'm off and running.

I've also been impressed with the simplicity of my car mechanic's multi-meter. For me, I graduated from an analog multi-meter to a digital multi-meter when I started testing the inner workings of computers. Now, I just look down and see 12.7 and I know I've got exactly 12.7 volts coming through. For my mechanic, he stepped backward from the digital world and simply stripped the two wires of a tail lamp that he keeps in his toolbox. He can touch those wires to the contacts, and BINGO! If it lights up, he's got juice! If it's a little dim, "Looks like the battery's weak."

My kids have gotten a taste of the simple life, too. Our home came equipped with a bidet in each bathroom. Well, our kids simply don't do things the French way, so the bidet has become a lot more useful as a kids' sink for hand washing. They've also been known to use it as a toy bathtub for their dolls. They've also plugged it with toilet paper. And they've watered the plants. And they've washed the floors, walls, books and anything else accessible. What a child-friendly apparatus! Come on over for a meal and you're bound to hear us say after supper, "Kids, go clean your dishes in the bidet before you go play!" Just don't let your mind wander too far on its intended use, and you can enjoy the simple life, too.

Life is different here, and that's just another Monday in the Middle East.

Flashback!
March 29, 1999 – ATV for You and Me

Driving in different countries is . . . well . . . different. Many of the laws that U.S. drivers would see as necessary for order and peace on the roads are not viewed with such high honor here. One such road rule is the matter of driving on one side of the road. As far as I have figured out, the law here is, "Don't hit anybody," and I can pretty much drive where I please.

Something else that adds to the fun is that there are no curbs or gutters on the roadsides. With rain during just one month of the year, what use would all of those gutters and curbs go to? This means that you don't need a Jeep to make your car into an off-road vehicle. For instance, last night as I was driving to a friend's house I saw the car in front of me veer off the road and head across a soccer field. That was the direction I needed to go, so rather than drive around the block using the streets, I followed suit and cut short my driving time. I suppose I had better be careful not to export these habits back to the States, though. I might just have a few hundred 5th and 6th graders chasing after me because of the tire tracks. What can I say? Life is different here, and that's just another Monday in the Middle East.

March 20, 2006 – The Middle East Oil Crisis

My memory of 1973 is a bit fuzzy, but many of you (*ahemm, ahemm*) middle-aged folks might recall the sudden 45% jump in gas prices as a result of the Middle East Oil Crisis. It seems strange that we are living atop a sea of oil here, but we've got our own little Middle East Oil Crisis these days. Now let me give you a bit of background here.

The United Arab Emirates is a sandy boat the size of Maine that buoys over 10% of the world's oil. Just considering the known oil reserves, the U.A.E. can easily continue to pump at today's maximum production rate 24 hours a day, 365 days a year *for the next hundred years!* Not a bad bit of income for a group of camel herders who lived mainly in tents just 50 years ago.

It's because of these huge reserves in oil that I was so surprised by a 30% jump in gas prices in one day. I mean really, isn't that one of the fringe benefits of living in the Arabian Gulf? "No taxes. Cheap gas." It reminds me of my Algebra II teacher in high school saying, "Why divide both sides by 2? Because you can!" Sounds like someone in an office here is saying, "Why raise prices on something we get for free? Because we can!"

Fortunately for us, the prices were jacked up only in the Emirates but not in neighboring Oman. We live right in the twilight zone between the two countries where three speed bumps constitute the border. Our small village of Buraimi, Oman, gives us cheap prices on daily living, and the neighboring city of Al Ain, U.A.E., gives us some taste of modernity, including high gas prices. Now the trick is this: Buraimi is equipped with three gas stations for its 80,000 residents. With that fact alone you might begin to sense the problem. I imagine my home town of Fond du Lac, Wisconsin, has at least 20 gas stations for it's 45,000 residents, but we make do with 3 here. So on September 1 of this past year when the U.A.E. sent its gas prices on an airplane ride, those 3 gas stations had to share with 400,000 Al Ain residents trying to save $15 per tank of gas for their gas-guzzling SUVs. Before we knew it, the scene looked like the 1970's complete with cars lined up for a quarter of a mile waiting to get gas. In fact, after getting a shipment of gas those 3 gas stations stay open for only a few hours before they are bone dry. Then, it's time to close up shop and wait another day or two before more gas arrives. There you have it: our own little Middle East Oil Crisis!

Life is different here, and that's just another Monday in the Middle East.

March 28, 2006 – Middle East Sick Day

Well, I had to call in sick yesterday. I'm an Arabic student, so I didn't call in sick to any gainful employment, but rather, I called in sick to Mondays in the Middle East. "No problem," you might say, which, when being translated into Swahili means, *Hakuna matata!* The Lion King popularized this concept, but The Lion King doesn't have taxis and taxis are what really give it meaning.

Hakuna matata is the African equivalent of what we call *Maalish* here in the Middle East. *Maalish* is a cardinal rule of life in the Middle East and it basically means "No worries!" or "No problem!" I was taught this principle before I even left the States for Egypt, but I didn't absorb its full effect until I had to use Cairo taxis. This particular day I needed to renew my tourist visa in downtown Redemption Square. The "tourist" visa is a strange beast; I know people who lived for ten years in Egypt as "tourists" because all they needed to do was show receipts that they'd spent at least $180 per month in the country. Tourism is the biggest source of hard currency for Egypt, so they make it pretty easy for foreigners to visit and even stay.

In any case, I absentmindedly showed up to renew my visa without my receipts which is no minor problem. So I raced down to the huge square to hail a taxi. I got a taxi all right, but the driver stopped right in the middle of traffic. "Whatever works for him works for me," I thought as I played real-life *Frogger* to get to the passenger-side door. I whipped open the door and threw my backpack in, only to hear a loud "CRUNCH!!" right behind me. I slowly looked around to see that another passing taxi had just smashed into the open passenger-side door! I then slowly turned my head to the driver of my taxi to hear his response, *"Maalish!"* The offending taxi driver said, *"Maalish?* Your door is smashed!" My taxi driver said again, *"Maalish!* No big deal! We go now."

I got out of the taxi at my destination and, sure enough, the door was a wee bit messed up. What could I do? I couldn't exactly pay for a door on the spot! In the end, I gave him a generous tip and took away a tip of generosity: *Maalish!* — Even when some American tourist just caused you several hundred dollars in car repairs. *Maalish!*

Life is different here, and that's just another Monday (Tuesday) in the Middle East.

Flashback!
March 15, 1999 – Dominoes Delivers

Back in the good old U.S. of A. ordering out for pizza is a special treat. A delicious pizza that someone else cooked can be enjoyed in the comfort of your own home with just a simple phone call. In Bahrain, we can still order out for pizza and enjoy the delicious pizza in our own home, but the matter of a simple phone call is a bit foreign to this land. Case in point: My wife called our local pizza place and requested a pizza. Murphy's Law would dictate that the person taking the order wouldn't understand a thing, and Murphy knows the Middle East. After giving our phone number multiple times, she also had to give the address multiple times even though it was already on file at the pizza place. Then she gave her best attempt at ordering a Hawaiian pizza with chicken wings while I sat chuckling to myself in another room. This whole shenanigan put serious doubt on whether we would actually get what we ordered. It's an event that makes one wonder if getting in the car and driving to the city center would actually get you what you want in about the same time you want it. I guess you could say life is different here, and that's just another Monday in the Middle East.

April 3, 2006 – Hitting the Links in the Middle East

I'm no Tiger Woods, but I love the game of golf. Maybe it's more that I love the *idea* of the game of golf because my golf ability is sorely lacking. Nonetheless, I had a good friend in Bahrain introduce me not only to Middle Eastern golf, but also to the business aspect of golf. "A lot can be accomplished on the golf course that simply would not happen in a board room," he said, and he proceeded over the next two hours to help me consider a job opportunity he had in mind for me. That's proof of concept for the business side of things, but the golf? Let's just say it's imaginative!

Now, there is a lot of sand in the Middle East. I'm sure you're aghast with surprise, but think about it: how do you play golf in sand with no grass? You carry your own grass, of course! Natural grass isn't too fond of the summer temperatures in the 110's-120's, so each player is equipped with a one-foot square of Astroturf. If you land in the sand that is marked as the fairway, you are allowed to pick up your ball, place it on your Astroturf, and play on. If you land in the "rough," the luxury of Astroturf is removed and you simply take your swing over the gravelly sand like I did most of the time.

So, two or three strokes later you've reached the green, right? Again, think "imagination!" The greens are actually "browns" that consist of fine sand mixed with oil aplenty and pounded smooth to sculpt the ground into something resembling a contoured golfing green. Think of the advantage with this: Tiger's shot would never come up short of the pin because of dew and wet grass!

I suppose the most imaginative aspect of Middle Eastern golf is the water hazards. How can you have a water hazard without water? Answer: rope, stakes, and a whole lot of imagination! So when I hit my ball into the water hazard, I used my prerogative to play it through instead of taking the one-stroke penalty. I stepped over the rope into the waist-deep pond (imagination!), took a smack at my ball that was deep in algae and mud (imagination!), and successfully played it onto the green in one shot. There you have it! Classic desert golf and definite proof that life is different here where it's just another Monday in the Middle East.

Printed in the United States
63853LVS00001B/1-240